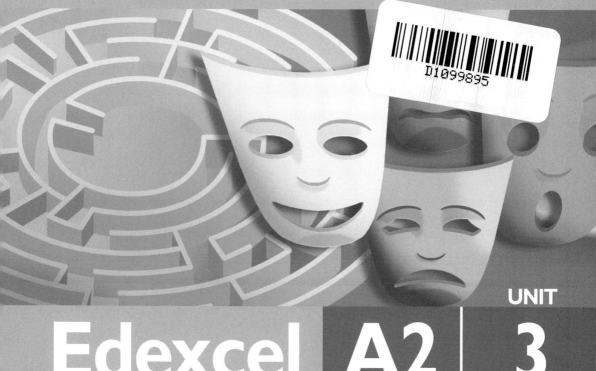

Edexcel A2

UNIT

3

Psychology

Health and Sport Psychology

Christine Brain

Philip Allan Updates, an imprint of Hodder Education, an Hachette UK company, Market Place, Deddington, Oxfordshire, OX15 0SE

Orders

Bookpoint Ltd, 130 Milton Park, Abingdon, Oxfordshire, OX14 4SB
tel: 01235 827720
fax: 01235 400454
e-mail: uk.orders@bookpoint.co.uk
Lines are open 9.00 a.m.–5.00 p.m., Monday to Saturday, with a 24-hour message answering service. You can also order through the Philip Allan Updates website: www.philipallan.co.uk

ISBN 978-0-340-94878-1

First printed 2010
Impression number 5 4 3 2 1
Year 2014 2013 2012 2011 2010

This guide has been written specifically to support students preparing for the Edexcel A2 Psychology Unit 3 examination. The content has been neither approved nor endorsed by Edexcel and remains the sole responsibility of the author.

Typeset by Phoenix Photosetting, Chatham, Kent
Printed by MPG Books, Bodmin

Hachette UK's policy is to use papers that are natural, renewable and recyclable products and made from wood grown in sustainable forests. The logging and manufacturing processes are expected to conform to the environmental regulations of the country of origin.

Contents

Introduction

■ ■ ■

Content Guidance

■ ■ ■

Questions and Answers

Sport psychology

Introduction

About this guide

This is a guide to two applications within Unit 3 of the Edexcel A2 specification: Health and Sport Psychology. Here is some good news (in the form of positive reinforcement). You can pass the exam for this unit, and you can do well. How can I draw this conclusion without knowing you? Because you are reading this guide.

Students who take the trouble to read this sort of guide:
- are motivated to do well
- have an idea about where to look for help
- understand what unit they are taking, and with which examination board
- know something about active learning — we can learn better if we engage in tasks, such as using this sort of student guide

So you already have some of the skills and knowledge you need — hence my claim that you can do well. However, this guide:
- is not a textbook — there is no substitute for reading the required material and taking notes
- does not tell you the actual questions on your paper, or give you the answers!

Aims of the guide

The aim of this guide is to provide you with a clear understanding of the requirements of Unit 3 of the A2 specification — focusing on two applications, as necessary for the unit — and to advise you on how best to meet these requirements.

This guide will look at:
- the psychology you need to know about
- what you need to be able to do and what skills you need
- how you could go about learning the necessary material
- what is being examined
- what you should expect in the examination for this application
- how you could tackle the different styles of exam question
- the format of the exam, including what questions might look like
- how questions are marked, including examples of answers, with examiner's comments

How to use this guide

A good way to use this guide is to read it through in the order in which it is presented. Alternatively, you can consider each topic in the Content Guidance section, and then turn to the relevant question in the Question and Answer section. Whichever way you use the guide, try some of the questions yourself to test your learning. You should know enough about the marking by this time to try to grade your own answers. If you are working with someone else, mark each other's answers.

The more you work on what is needed, the better. Have other textbooks available too — you will need access to all the relevant information.

How to learn the material

- Make notes, be concise and use your own notes for final revision.
- Have a separate sheet of paper for each application.
- For each application, note down the five headings (definitions, methodology, content, studies in detail and key issue/practical) and use them as a guide. Leave room to fit your notes in under each heading.
- Read through each section, then make notes as needed (very briefly).
- Be sure to make notes on evaluation points.
- Finally, note down briefly three things about a key issue that describe the issue, and six 'facts' linking concepts to the issue.

Another useful method is to use cards for each topic. Have the topic heading on one side of the card and brief notes on the other. Remember to note down equal amounts of knowledge and evaluation.

Study skills and revision strategies

If you have been studying the Unit 3 material on Health and/or Sport Psychology, and have engaged in a reasonable amount of learning up to now, you can make good use of this guide.

This guide can also help if you know very little of the material and have only a short time before the examination. If this describes you, you have a lot of work and long hours of study ahead — but you can do it.

Before reading on, answer the following questions:
- How long is left before the exam?
- Do you have a revision plan?
- Are you sure you want to pass, and hopefully do well? Renewing your motivation can help.
- Are you stressed and in a panic?
- Can you stick to your plan, and trust it?

If you need to, draw up a revision plan now, remind yourself that you do want to succeed, and practise some relaxation techniques.

Revision plan

- Start at least 4 weeks before the exam date (sooner if possible).
- Using times that suit you (6 a.m. might be a great time to study!), draw up a blank timetable for each of the weeks.
- On the timetable, fill in all your urgent commitments (cancel as many plans as you can).
- Divide up what is left, allocating slots to all your subjects as appropriate. Don't forget to build in meal times, breaks and time for sleep.
- Stick to the plan if at all possible, but if you have to, amend it as you go.
- When studying, have frequent, short rests and no distractions.

Time management

Answer the following questions to see how good you are at time management.

(1) Are you usually punctual?

yes   no

(2) Do you tend to work fast and then correct mistakes?

yes   no

(3) Do you often put things off?

yes   no

(4) Do you feel stressed because you never have enough time?

yes   no

(5) Do you work slowly and carefully, and try to get things right first time?

yes   no

(6) Do you daydream?

yes   no

(7) Are you forgetful?

yes   no

(8) Do you find it hard to get started?

yes   no

(9) Do you keep your desk tidy?

yes   no

Score 0 for 'yes' and 1 for 'no' to questions 1, 5 and 9. Score 1 for 'yes' and 0 for 'no' to questions 2, 3, 4, 6, 7 and 8. A score of 3 or below means your time management is quite good; a score of 4 and above means you need to work on it.

Relaxation techniques

The boxes below suggest some ways to relax. Use these as appropriate.

Technique 1 — takes about 10 minutes

This technique is useful at the start or end of a longish revision period.

- Lie on the floor and make yourself comfortable.
- Working from toes to head, tense each of your muscles in turn and then relax.
- Having relaxed your body, now relax your thoughts.
- Take yourself in your mind to a place where you feel at peace — this could be a favourite holiday place, or a favourite place on a walk. Closing your eyes will help.
- Have a good look around (mentally!), sit down there and listen to the sounds of the place.
- Stay there and try not to come back yet.
- When you are ready, come back. Slowly start to hear the sounds around you, and lie with your body relaxed for a little while longer.

Technique 2 — takes about 5 minutes

This technique is useful as you revise. Work for between 30 minutes and an hour, and then stop to relax as follows:

- Sit comfortably and try to ignore anything going on around you.
- Imagine you are in a barn, sitting on the rafters under the roof, swinging your legs and sitting comfortably. Closing your eyes will help.
- Now, imagine that the barn has open doors at both ends, and there is a river rushing through from one end of the barn to the other. You are sitting swinging your legs, watching the river rush through below you.
- Hear the water rushing through, sit comfortably, and just watch.
- Think of the water as your thoughts rushing away.
- You are not involved, just watching.
- After about 3 minutes or when you are ready, slowly start to hear the sounds around you, and gradually bring your thoughts back into the real world. Look around you for a minute or two and check that you feel better, before getting back to work.

Technique 3 — takes about 1 minute

This technique is useful when you are actually in the examination, and can be used if you are too anxious to continue.
- Imagine you are in an exam now.
- Imagine that you are getting anxious.
- Pick up a pen as if to write.
- Hold the pen up in front of you and stare at it.
- Let all your other thoughts go and think about the pen.
- Try to think of nothing else even for a few seconds.
- Get back to work!

Examination structure and skills

Unit 3 consists of four applications of psychology: criminological, child, health and sport psychology. You must select *two* of these applications to study and you will have to answer questions on both of them in the exam. This study guide looks at two of them — health and sport psychology. Another study guide looks at the other two.

There will be one whole question for each application, which will be divided into separate parts. Each application covers five areas: definitions, methodology, content, studies in detail and key issue/practical. There will not be a question for each area of the application — questions for each application will range across these five areas.

Exam structure and assessment objectives (AOs)

Each of the two A2 exam papers (Units 3 and 4) has some short answer questions, some extended writing questions and finally a 12-mark extended writing question (essay question) at the end.

The assessment objectives (AOs) of the A2 exam papers are the same as for the AS papers. Briefly, they are as follows (they are explained more fully below):
- AO1 — testing knowledge with understanding and good communication skills
- AO2 — testing evaluation, assessment and applications
- AO3 — testing understanding and evaluation of methodology, including other people's studies

Don't think that someone sets each paper with past papers in front of them, avoiding what has been asked before. Imagine someone trying to set an interesting paper, covering a range of topics from the five areas for each application, and balancing AO1, AO2 and AO3 marks according to the required percentages of each.

It is not possible to guess what will be on the paper — don't try. Prepare answers for all possible questions. The only guarantee is that there will be the two types of question (short answer and extended writing) and an essay question at the end of each paper; and you can expect the mark allocation for that essay to be 12 marks.

Different people set the papers, and there are not as many strict rules about setting the papers as you might think. Tips in this guide include words such as 'usually'. Each paper will be different, and you have to be prepared to answer whatever questions appear. For example, there are many ways that short answer questions can be written, such as:

- 'Explain what is meant by...'
- 'Describe the procedure of...'
- 'Outline the theory...'
- 'Outline two weaknesses of...'
- 'What is the hypothesis in this study?'

Read the question carefully and do what is asked, and you will do well.

Assessment objectives in more detail

The assessment objectives are listed in the specification. A brief explanation is given below, but check the full list of what you will be assessed on.

Assessment Objective 1: knowledge and understanding (AO1)

- You need to recognise, recall and show understanding of psychological know-ledge, including theories, studies, methods and concepts, as well as psychological principles, perspectives and applications.
- You must communicate clearly and effectively, and present and select material well. For example, if you are asked to explain what is meant by tolerance (health psychology) for 2 marks, and you just say that it is about getting used to a drug, you have not explained anything. You need to make your points clearly — for example:

'Tolerance means that the body gets used to the amount of a drug that is being used (e.g. alcohol), and this means that to get the same effect more of the drug is needed, so more and more is used. This goes up to a certain level and generally then levels out.'

- You may lose marks by using bullet points, so avoid them. The problem with bullet points is that they encourage shorthand, meaning that your answer will not be clearly and effectively communicated.

Assessment Objective 2: evaluation and comment (AO2)

You must be able to:

- analyse and evaluate psychological theories and concepts, referring to relevant evidence
- apply psychological knowledge and understanding to unfamiliar situations
- assess the validity, reliability and credibility of psychological knowledge

Assessment Objective 3: description and evaluation of how psychology works (AO3)

You must:

- be able to describe ethical, safe and skilful practical techniques and processes, including selecting appropriate qualitative and quantitative methods
- know how to make, record and communicate reliable and valid measurements, using primary and secondary sources
- be able to analyse, explain, interpret and evaluate methodology, results and impact of both your own practicals and the studies of others

The Unit 3 exam

Unit 3 is assessed in a 90-minute exam. Answers are written in a booklet similar to those used at GCSE. There are 60 marks available. This means you need to score around 1 mark per minute, with 30 minutes to spare for reading and thinking. In general, you can expect to gain 1 mark for each point that answers the question, or for elaboration of a point. Answers must be communicated 'clearly and effectively' (see AO1 above). Avoid one-word answers unless they are asked for. The final essay question is expected to be worth 12 marks.

Overall, marks are awarded as follows:

- About 30% of the marks (around 18 marks when considering both applications) are awarded for knowledge and understanding (AO1).
- About 40% (around 24 marks when considering both applications) are for evaluation and comment and application to unfamiliar situations (AO2).
- About 30% (around 18 marks when considering both applications) are for knowledge and assessment of practical work, both your own and other people's.

In practice you can simply focus on revising equal amounts of AO1, AO2 and AO3 (knowledge, evaluation and practical work) and answer each question as it arises.

Two types of marking

There are two types of marking. One type is point-based marking, where 1 mark is awarded per point made, and there are also marks for elaboration of a point. The other type of marking involves 'levels', which means there are bands of marks that are awarded according to the quality of the answer. An example is the following mark scheme for a question asking for the IV for a study for 2 marks:

- 0 marks — no appropriate material (e.g. giving the DV)
- 1 mark — not fully operationalised (e.g. giving one side of the IV)
- 2 marks — fully operationalised, giving both or all sides of the IV, and possibly an example

Questions about your own practicals are marked according to levels and quality — for example, if you are asked about planning your content analysis, a thorough answer will get full marks and a weak answer will get very few marks.

The essays are also marked using levels and according to quality. For example, if you are asked about two ways of improving performance (sport psychology) and you only discuss one way you will be in the middle band somewhere. It is in the levels marking that your writing skills are assessed, including how well you select material for your answer, and the quality of your spelling, grammar and use of terminology.

AO1, AO2 and AO3: getting it right

You must be sure to answer the question that is set — you should then cover the AO1, AO2 and/or AO3 skills. The key words in the question (e.g. 'outline'), called **injunctions**, guide what you need to write. If you answer the question, you will automatically do what is required without worrying about the various assessment objectives.

Table 1 shows some examples of how AO1 injunctions are used and Table 2 shows examples of AO2 injunctions. Table 3 shows some examples of AO3 questions, which can include various kinds of injunctions but must be about practicals and methodology in some way. Note that it is not so much the word itself (e.g. 'describe') as the whole question that makes it AO1, AO2 or AO3. The figures in brackets suggest the mark allocation you might expect for such a question.

Table 1 Examples of AO1 questions/injunctions

Type of question	What is being asked for
Describe a theory... (5)	Say what something is (a theory in this case). Imagine describing the theory to someone who knows little about the subject.
Identify a theory... (1)	Give enough information so that the examiner can understand what is being referred to. For example, if asked to identify a theory of motivation, the answer might be 'Atkinson and McClelland'.
Identify a study... (1)	Name either the study or the psychologist(s). For example, if the question asks for a study, the answer might be 'Boyd and Munroe' or 'the "climbers' imagery" study'.
Outline a definition of the ... application (3)	Follow the instructions for 'describe', but remember that this injunction requires less detail, and hence carries fewer marks.

Table 2 Examples of AO2 questions/injunctions

Type of question	What is being asked for
Outline a strength of... (2)	You are asked to outline something, so the injunction seems to be AO1 (i.e. knowledge and understanding). However, as what is outlined is a *strength* (in this case), and thus you are being asked to evaluate something, this question would carry AO2 marks.
With regard to the stimulus material above, explain... (6)	You are asked to refer to some stimulus material and apply your knowledge of psychology to explain the material in some way. Refer to the material at least once in your answer.

Compare two explanations for substance misuse… (6)	You are asked to choose two explanations for substance misuse and then write about how they are similar and/or how they are different.
Assess how far a campaign against using recreational drugs is successful… (4)	You are asked to consider one campaign and suggest how successful it is. You should also identify any ways in which it is unsuccessful, so you can come to an overall conclusion about its success. Focus on success, given the question.

Table 3 Examples of AO3 questions/injunctions

Type of question	What is being asked for
Outline the aim(s) of your article/content analysis… (2)	You are asked to say what the purpose of your study was; that is, to say briefly what you were trying to find out. 'Outline' sounds like an AO1 injunction, but as this is about your practical, it is an AO3 question.
Evaluate one of these studies — either Cottrell et al. (1968), Koivula (1995) or Craft et al. (2003). (5)	You will have covered one of these studies but probably not all of them. Choose the one you know and give comments, criticisms, good points and so on. Consider strengths and weaknesses of the research method, perhaps, or make criticisms of the ethics involved. Look at alternative findings or consider whether justified conclusions are drawn. Although 'evaluate' sounds like an AO2 injunction, the question is about someone else's study, which is psychology in practice, so it is an AO3 question. However, it could be used on an AO2 one.

Conclusions: use of injunctions and the AO1/AO2/AO3 split

Don't just think of a word in the question as being the whole question. For example, you might think 'describe' is an AO1 command because it seems to ask for knowledge. However, 'describe a strength…' is an AO2 injunction because it asks for evaluation; and 'describe the procedure of your practical' is an AO3 question because it asks about psychology in practice. 'Discuss' could signal AO2 marks if you are asked to 'discuss the usefulness of…': because you are considering how useful something is, you are doing more than showing knowledge about it. The best approach is to *answer the question*. If you pay careful attention to the question so that you understand what it asks you to do, all should be well.

The specification gives a list of what injunction words mean in your course so you could look at that to check your understanding. However, the question should indicate clearly what you have to do. Remember that the specification, sample papers and sample mark scheme are on the Edexcel website.

Table 4 on page 14 shows how marks are split between the assessment objectives for each unit of the A-level.

Table 4 Approximate mark allocation AO1/AO2/AO3 for the whole A-level

	AO1	AO2	AO3	Total
AS Unit 1	8%	6%	6%	20%
AS Unit 2	12%	9%	9%	30%
A2 Unit 3	6%	8%	6%	20%
A2 Unit 4	9%	14%	7%	30%
Total	**35%**	**37%**	**28%**	**100%**

You can see that, for the two AS units, you were assessed more on your knowledge and understanding (40%) than on your ability to comment and evaluate (30%). For Unit 3, you will be assessed more on your ability to comment and evaluate (40%) than on your knowledge and understanding (30%). For Unit 4, your knowledge and understanding and your evaluation and comment skills are assessed differently as well, with AO1 taking up 30% of the unit and AO2 taking up 47% of the unit. So the two A2 units have noticeably more AO2 than AO1, with AO3 staying roughly the same.

Essentially, then, you have to learn material so you know and understand it, and then plan some criticisms, comments and evaluation points. As a rule of thumb, be sure to learn or plan as many evaluation and comment points as you learn information points.

Differences between AS and A2

Although a lot of what is true for AS still applies to A2 — for example, the AO1, AO2 and AO3 assessment objectives — the A2 exams require higher-level skills.

At A2, more marks are given for AO2 (evaluation and comment) than for AO1 (knowledge and understanding). This is different from what is required at AS. It means you need to comment, evaluate, assess, consider strengths, and so on, more than you need to give information. When you are making notes and preparing answers to exam questions, remember to concentrate on criticisms. Whenever you read an evaluation point, note it down and learn it.

Greater depth is also required in your answers at A2. For example, you could be asked about two explanations for individual differences in sporting participation. The specification does not say that you need studies and evidence, but they could be useful. Remember to refer to the assessment objectives outlined in this introduction. The specification might not ask you specifically to learn studies regarding the inverted U hypothesis (you are asked to describe and evaluate the inverted U hypothesis for sport psychology), but you will need to refer to relevant evidence to support your answers (AO2). Psychology is built on evidence from studies, so when revising it is useful to have a list of names of studies and a brief outline of what each is about. Note also that Unit 3 is about applications of psychology, so be ready to apply your knowledge.

Content
Guidance

This section provides an overview of what you need to learn for the Health Psychology and Sport Psychology applications of Unit 3. It includes some AO1 (knowledge and understanding) material for each topic as well as AO2 evaluation points. There are also AO3 points, which are about methodology and how science and psychology work. Each application is divided into the following areas:

- Definition of the application
- Methodology and how science works
- Content
- Studies in detail
- Evidence in practice: key issue and practical

The overview provided for each application starts with a summary of what you need to know, before covering each of the above five areas in turn.

Note that when studying your two applications, you must include one analysis of articles and one content analysis. In this study guide the Health Psychology application has the article analysis and the Sport Psychology application has the content analysis.

Health psychology
Summary of what you need to know

> **Tip**
>
> In this study guide, choices are made for you, to limit the material. However, if you have studied a different choice it is probably better to revise that, rather than learn something new at this stage.

Definition of the application

You need to be able to:
- define what the application is about (what is meant by health psychology)
- define key terms, including substance misuse, synapse, tolerance, physical dependence, psychological dependence, withdrawal

Methodology and how science works

You need to be able to:
- describe and evaluate the use of animals in laboratory studies when researching into drugs
- describe and evaluate two methods using humans to study the effects of drugs

When evaluating you need to consider their relative strengths and weaknesses — including, with regard to animals, practical and ethical strengths and weaknesses, and, with regard to humans, issues of reliability and validity.

Content

You need to be able to do the following.
- Describe and compare the relative strengths and weaknesses of two explanations of substance misuse — one a biological explanation and one a learning explanation. In this book neuronal transmission is chosen as the biological explanation and social learning theory as the learning explanation.
- Describe, with reference to heroin and another drug (chosen from alcohol, cocaine, ecstasy, marijuana and nicotine), the following: mode of action, effects, tolerance, physical dependence, psychological dependence and withdrawal. In this book nicotine (smoking) is chosen as the other drug.
- Describe and evaluate drug treatment for heroin dependence and another treatment for substance misuse. In this book token economy is chosen as the other treatment.
- Describe and evaluate one campaign against the use of recreational drugs. In this book the British Heart Foundation (2008) campaign against smoking is chosen.

Studies in detail

You need to learn two studies in detail, one of which must be Blättler et al. (2002). The other must be a study on alcohol, cocaine, ecstasy, marijuana or nicotine. In this book Ennett et al. (1994) is chosen as the other study in detail because nicotine is the other drug chosen.

Evidence in practice: key issue and practical

You need to be able to describe one key issue within the application (an issue that uses content from the application) and conduct a practical on it. In this study guide the issue of how drug abuse can be treated is chosen for the key issue and the focus for the practical.

> **Tip**
>
> The content is necessarily summarised here — add more detail yourself.

Definition of the application

This section looks at some of the key terms and what health psychology is about.

Health psychology focuses on areas of health where mental processes are involved, such as sleep, stress, drug misuse, how people cope with life-threatening illnesses, and mental disorders. The focus is on preventing problems from arising, including prevention of risk taking and unhealthy behaviour, as well as on helping people after they have health problems.

Health psychologists help to promote healthy behaviour, focusing not only on physical aspects such as healthy eating and exercise, but also on social aspects such as social support and family relationships. In general the focus is on a biopsychosocial model, where biological factors are combined with psychological and social ones, and it is accepted that all three contribute to health and to ill health. For example, bereavement is recognised as possibly leading to problems with health, and counselling might be offered to try to alleviate the effects of grieving.

Health psychology is a large area of study and your course focuses on substance misuse. Key terms you need to be able to define include substance misuse (p. 25), synapse (p. 25), tolerance (p. 28), physical dependence (pp. 28–29), psychological dependence (p. 29) and withdrawal (p. 29). These are all defined within the methodology and content sections that follow.

> **Tip**
>
> A good way of extending a definition, when there are 3 marks available, is to add an example.

Methodology and how science works

This section looks at laboratory experiments using animals and two research methods using humans, giving description and evaluation. The focus is on studies looking at substance misuse.

Animal laboratory studies looking at substance misuse

Animal laboratory studies have the features of laboratory studies in general, including careful controls of all aspects except the variables to be manipulated and those to be measured:

- There will be an independent variable (IV) that is manipulated when all other variables are kept the same.
- The IV is manipulated in order to see the effect of a dependent variable (DV) that is measured.
- Controls include environment, type of animal and state of animal.
- Cause-and-effect conclusions are aimed at.
- Scientific equipment can be used to help with controls and measurement.

Animal laboratory studies are used to look at drugs such as those listed for your course, including heroin and nicotine, the two drugs covered in this study guide.

The link between drug use and kidney disease

Kidneys can fail to function properly (renal disease) and this has been linked to drug use. Animal studies suggest that renal disease is connected more to cocaine than to heroin use and this suggests that the drug itself is important (that not all drugs lead to renal disease). Mice are given either heroin or cocaine in various doses and their renal function is tested. All other factors are kept the same. The drug (heroin or cocaine) is the IV and the renal functioning is the DV.

Evaluation

Strengths

- Studies using animals in laboratory conditions are replicable because of the carefully controlled conditions and procedures, so reliability can be tested for.
- Studies giving cause-and-effect, scientific conclusions have more weight and conclusions are seen as stronger because of issues such as objectivity and lack of interpretation in the findings.

Weaknesses

- Other studies, not animal experiments, have found that economic conditions, culture and behaviour were more likely to relate to renal disease then heroin (e.g. Jaffe and Kimmer 2006), which suggests that such experiments do not tell the whole story.
- Experiments tend not to be valid, as the above point suggests, because (due to the careful controls) only one factor is studied, whereas renal disease is likely to have other causes apart from, or as well as, drug usage.

- Animal studies also tend not to be valid — generalising from animals to humans might not give valid results because humans and animals are different.

Drugs as reinforcers

Meisch (2001) used animals in laboratory conditions and looked at the animals taking the drugs themselves (oral self-administration). For example, rhesus monkeys were given the chance to take the drug to see if they would do so — the question was whether the drug was rewarding enough to be taken again and this would then focus on addiction (based on the idea of operant conditioning). Drugs were not just recreational drugs such as opioids, but also barbiturates and other such drugs. Such studies have to try to take into account whether the animal likes the taste of the drug or not (which is different from saying that the effects of the drug are reinforcing). Such studies show that monkeys will choose to take the drug rather than water, which does suggest it is a reward and reinforcing.

Evaluation

Strengths

- Monkeys and humans share many of their genes, so generalising from such findings to say they are true of humans seems reasonable.
- Humans do seem to become addicted to certain drugs because of their effects, so the study findings reinforce what is known about human drug use, which adds validity.

Weaknesses

- Monkeys are not human, and humans have more problem-solving abilities and consciousness, for example, so perhaps it is not reasonable to generalise from monkey behaviour to human behaviour.
- Ethical issues could be raised about using monkeys in this way, though if ethical guidelines are followed this might not be a problem.

Tips

- Use AS material about using animals in research as well as AS material about operant conditioning.
- Use examples of animal studies on drug usage to illustrate the method, as well as using description points about the research method itself.

Evaluation of animal laboratory experiments

Animal laboratory studies can be evaluated in terms of practical and ethical issues, and also in terms of validity, reliability and generalisability.

Practical issues

Strengths

- Animals are relatively small and easy to handle.
- Animals can have short gestation periods and reproductive cycles so generations can be studied more easily.
- Some animals have a similar brain structure to humans (e.g. mice).
- Animals can be more strongly controlled than humans as there are fewer ethical objections, and so findings can be more objective.

Weaknesses
- Animals' brains are not the same as human brains, and neither is their genetic structure the same as that of humans.
- Human behaviour is complex, so isolating one variable might not give valid data.
- There is a lack of credibility about using findings from animal studies and saying they are true of humans because of the differences.

Ethical issues

Strengths
- It could be said to be more ethical to use animals than humans in some studies, such as when operations are required, which can happen when studying drugs and wanting to set up a measured dosage.
- Some say we must do all we can for our own species regardless of whether other species are harmed.
- Animals can benefit from the findings of some animal laboratory studies.
- There are strong guidelines to be followed and government backing for the guidelines.

Weaknesses
- Guidelines are there to stop too much discomfort but animals can still be hurt and feel pain, so some question whether such research should be done at all.
- Humans are animals so we should not do to animals what we would not do to humans.

Validity

Animal experiments are likely to have a lack of validity because of the unnatural elements in the situation.
- The laboratory setting is unnatural, which means lack of ecological validity is likely.
- What is done is also likely to be unnatural, so the findings might lack validity.
- However, sometimes there is validity — perhaps the situation of animals taking drugs orally represents drug-taking sufficiently for findings about rewarding effects of the drugs to be valid.

Reliability

Animal experiments are likely to have reliable findings because they can be replicated — and will be replicated before findings are published.
- The controlled conditions and procedures will be replicable, for example.
- Measures will be objective and scientific, so can be done again, for example.
- However, animals are living unpredictable beings, perhaps, at least in some cases, so each study might show individual differences.

Generalisability

Animal experiments could be said to lack generalisability, but on the other hand there might be some generalisability claimed.
- Animals are not human beings and do not have the same levels of consciousness or exactly the same brain structure or function, so generalisability is perhaps not possible.

- There are different types of animals, some similar to humans, some not, so talking about animal laboratory studies covers studies that might not be generalisable and others where findings might be more generalisable.

Two research methods using humans to study the effect of drugs

The two research methods considered here are interviewing and questionnaires.

Tip

You may have studied different research methods for this section (e.g. more biological methods such as scanning), in which case you might like to revise them instead of learning something different at this stage.

Interviewing

- Interviews can be structured, semi-structured or unstructured.
- Structured interviews have set questions that everyone answers; unstructured interviews have a schedule, but the actual questions can vary according to how the interview progresses.
- Semi-structured interviews include some set questions and some areas where issues can be explored.
- Often interviews involve both qualitative data from open questioning and quantitative data from closed questioning, but there is often more focus on gathering qualitative data.
- An example of a study using interviewing is Blättler et al. (2002) (pp. 34–35), where it was used to find out about cocaine use in heroin addicts on a drug treatment programme.

Evaluation of interviewing as a research method

Strengths	Weaknesses
Interviewing can be in-depth, so data are likely to be valid because different issues can be explored (depending on the type of interview).	Interviewers may influence responses by the way they dress, or their age or gender. This would affect reliability, as another interviewer might get different results.
Interviewing can gain valid data because participants can use their own wording and are not as restricted as with questionnaires.	The data have to be analysed, which can be subjective as there may be a lot of qualitative data to be put into themes. These can come from the researcher's preconceived ideas rather than from the data. If analysis is subjective, another researcher might analyse the results differently, so there would not be reliability.

> **Tip**
>
> Use the procedure of Blättler et al. (2002) as an example of the use of interviewing in the study of heroin and its effects.

Questionnaires

- Questionnaires tend to involve both open and closed questions.
- Closed questions give quantitative data and can derive percentages for comparison purposes.
- Open questions give qualitative data and depth and detail, which can be used to generate hypotheses for testing in another study.
- Questionnaires can done by post, in groups or face to face.
- An example of a study using questionnaires is Ennett et al. (1994) (pp. 36–37), which used them to find out about the smoking habits of young people and also about their friendship groups.

Evaluation of questionnaires as a research method

Strengths	Weaknesses
They can be reliable because the same clear questions are set for everyone, with the same instructions.	The fixed questions can limit validity because people must answer what is asked and may miss important areas of enquiry.
There should be no bias, such as response set, because of careful planning and the use of a pilot study. With no bias, if the study were to be carried out again, the same results would be found, making the results reliable.	There can be social desirability if people answer how they think they are supposed to answer. Therefore, answers would not be valid because they are not 'real life' answers about genuine beliefs and behaviour.

> **Tip**
>
> Use the procedure of Ennett et al. (1994) as an example of the use of questionnaires to study substance misuse — in this case the effect of peers on smoking behaviour.

Human studies into the effects of drugs

Blättler et al. (2002) (pp. 34–35) used interviewing and other research methods such as urine testing to look at heroin and cocaine use, and Ennett et al. (1994) (pp. 36–37) used questionnaires to find out whether there was a link between friendship groups and smoking behaviour. These are the two studies used as studies in detail for this application, so are covered in good depth in a later section (pp. 34–37). Use these two studies as examples of studies into the effects of drugs. Ennett et al. is more about what affects the use of drugs rather than the effects of drugs, but you could say that taking drugs affects friendship groups, so the study fits the course here.

Evaluation of using humans to study drugs

Research methods can be evaluated in terms of how valid and how reliable they are.

Validity

- Interviews can obtain valid data because they usually explore issues in depth, and unstructured interviews in particular allow the respondent to lead the interview and to say what they want to say.
- Structured interviews can lack validity if they force answers and, perhaps by doing so, omit certain areas that need to be explored.
- Questionnaires can give demand characteristics if the respondent guesses the answer that is required or goes against what they think is required, leading to a lack of validity.
- Questionnaires can be affected by social desirability, which means the respondent says what they think they ought to say, leading to a lack of validity.
- It is hard to study drug usage and the effects of drugs because of the many factors that seem to be involved, such as peer group, environment and culture.

Reliability

- Unstructured interviews tend to lack reliability, as they are hard to compare if they cover in-depth areas guided by each respondent differently.
- Structured interviews are more replicable, so they can be tested for reliability and the findings compared.
- Questionnaires can be repeated because the questions are set and many are closed questions, so there can be reliability.

Generalisability

- Unstructured interviews focus on individuals and an in-depth study of them, for example of their drug-taking behaviour. It is hard to generalise from such individual and unique findings, though the interview schedule can guide the coverage sufficiently so that each interview is similar enough to allow comparison and generalisation.
- Sampling is what affects generalisability: if the sample of participants who agree to be interviewed or to do a questionnaire is broad enough, then generalisation might be possible.

 Tip

Use your AS learning about questionnaires and interviews (in the social approach).

Content

This section looks at five areas:

- two explanations for substance misuse
- comparisons between biological and learning explanations of substance misuse
- two drugs in detail — how heroin and nicotine work
- two ways of treating substance misuse
- campaigns against the use of recreational drugs

Two explanations for substance misuse

Drugs are mind-altering substances and **substance misuse** (a key term) refers to the use of a drug in a way that affects the individual's mental and physical health. The use of a drug is 'abuse' or 'misuse' when it interferes with social and personal functioning. Some drugs, such as barbiturates, are prescribed for physical and/or mental health problems, and other drugs are called **'recreational drugs'** because they are taken purely for pleasure. This section focuses on recreational drugs, in particular heroin and nicotine. Two explanations for substance misuse are considered here: the biological one of how heroin works in the brain and the learning one of how drug use is affected by social learning and role models.

> ### Tips
> - If you covered different explanations in your course you might prefer to revise those, rather than to learn new ones.
> - Use your knowledge of the biological approach and the learning approach (social learning theory) from the AS course when describing and evaluating the explanations for drug misuse.

A biological explanation: neuronal transmission

One biological explanation for drug misuse rests on the idea of how the drug works in the brain. Neuronal transmission can explain why there is a pleasure response and why there is a tolerance effect (where more of the drug is needed to get the same pleasure response, up to a certain quantity).

Like a neurotransmitter, a drug acts at the receptors of a neuron. This happens at the **synapse** (a key term), which is the gap between the receptors of one neuron and the terminal buttons of another. A drug (recreational or medical) can be taken up by the relevant receptors of a neuron, or the drug can block receptors so that uptake of a neurotransmitter does not take place. For example, heroin works like morphine — it acts on opioid receptors and this activity causes changes at the receptors.

The receptors of two neurotransmitters, dopamine and serotonin, are involved in drug misuse and addiction; both these neurotransmitters are linked to pleasure and positive emotions. For example, cocaine directly stimulates the dopamine receptors, increases available dopamine messages and so gives pleasurable feelings. Opioids like heroin slow down brain activity and uptake of neurotransmitters so dopamine messages stay active for longer, again giving pleasurable feelings. People continue to take the drug to get the pleasurable feelings, which explains drug misuse.

There may be more to it as some people may, for example, have underdeveloped dopamine or serotonin systems and so would seek more pleasure and be more likely to turn to drug use. This could explain why some people are more likely to become addicted than others.

Evaluation

Strengths
- PET scans have shown that neuronal activity when someone is smoking a 'normal' cigarette is different from when someone is smoking a low-nicotine one. This suggests that neuronal activity is affected by nicotine and is evidence for the biological explanation.
- Animal studies show that different drugs affect receptors in different ways, which is evidence for the biological explanation. Also, as such studies can be repeated, reliability of the findings can be shown.

Weaknesses
- Animal studies have findings that might not apply to humans.
- PET scans seem to show valid behaviour because they involve real behaviour, but the situation is still artificial so the findings might lack validity.

A social learning explanation

Social learning theory suggests that people learn by observing role models and then imitating their behaviour. The individual observes, pays attention, remembers and then imitates, if motivated to do so. The role model is likely to be someone similar to the individual and also someone the individual identifies with. Role models can be parents or peers — both fit with the social learning theory and with the evidence. Baer et al. (1987) found that both parents and peers were likely to be role models in general, so it makes sense to say this is true for drug misuse behaviour as well.

Positive reinforcement is part of social learning theory too — that people continue with behaviour they are positively reinforced for — so praise or being seen as part of a group, for example, is likely to maintain the behaviour.

Younger adults seem more susceptible than older adults, high-status people have a stronger influence in general and also the particular drug goes with the peer-group influence.

Vicarious learning can help to explain why, though taking a drug (e.g. smoking or drinking alcohol) for the first time is a bad experience, people do it again. If they see others (such as parents and friends) enjoying the experience, then they are more likely to repeat the behaviour.

Evaluation

Strengths
- Bandura and others have shown the effects of social learning, such as behaviour modelled by adults and repeated (in laboratory conditions) by others. So there is a lot of reliable evidence that people imitate role models and what they observe, including evidence for vicarious learning.
- Social learning has been shown in animals: for example, when monkeys show fear of a harmless object other monkeys show fear of it as well, just through observing the fear of others.

Weaknesses
- Ennett et al. (1994) (pp. 36–37) showed that friendship cliques and smoking did not go together. In their study, smoking did not seem to be the result of people conforming to peer behaviour. This goes against social learning theory.
- It is hard to show a cause-and-effect link between observed behaviour and acting out of the behaviour. For example, parents can be role models but they might also pass on a gene linked with addiction.

Comparing biological and learning approach explanations for substance misuse

The biological and learning explanations can be evaluated by comparing them and looking at similarities and weaknesses.

Nature–nurture

A biological explanation is about nature: for example, neuronal transmission is how the brain works for everyone, and people are born with a brain that functions in this way. A learning explanation, however, is about nurture: for example, people imitate role models in their environment and drug use can come from observing parents taking drugs. So the two explanations differ with regard to the nature–nurture debate.

Validity

A biological explanation and a social learning explanation are both hard to test for validity as much of the evidence comes from experiments, often in the laboratory. The setting is not real life, such as smokers smoking either 'normal' cigarettes or low-nicotine ones. As the setting is not real the findings may not be valid, because the brain functioning might be affected by the strange setting and task. Social learning theory comes from laboratory experiments where adults act aggressively or children watch aggressive films and the behaviour is observed. This is not a natural situation. However, it could be argued that watching aggression, such as on television, is a naturally occurring situation, so social learning theory findings are likely to be demonstrated to be more valid than a biological explanation.

Reliability

As both the biological and social learning explanations rest on experimental evidence, studies are replicable and have been done again with the same results. So both explanations have reliability.

Two drugs in detail

Heroin and nicotine are the two drugs covered in this section.

> **Tips**
> - If you covered a different drug from nicotine you might prefer to revise that rather than learn about a new drug here.
> - The Blättler et al. (2002) study is about heroin addiction and the Ennett et al. (1994) study is about smoking behaviour. It is useful to study a treatment for smoking as well

as a campaign against heroin or smoking, so that you can use different parts of your learning for different questions. It would also be useful to choose a key issue based around heroin or nicotine/smoking, as is done here.

Heroin

This section looks at heroin, specifically its mode of action and effects, and how tolerance, dependence and withdrawal work with regard to heroin.

Mode of action

'Mode of action' refers to how the drug works in the brain and at the synapse.

- Heroin is an opiate, which acts as a depressant and painkiller in the central nervous system.
- Heroin is converted into morphine in the brain and the morphine then acts at the opioid receptors in the brain.
- The drug changes the action of dopamine in the reward pathway of the brain, releasing more dopamine than usual.
- The morphine binds (fits) to the receptors to reduce inhibitory effects on dopamine receptors so there is more dopamine activity.
- The release of dopamine gives a 'high' — a pleasurable feeling.

Tip

Use this explanation of the mode of action of heroin as an example when explaining the biological explanation for drug misuse.

Effects

Short-term effects include pleasure and the 'rush' of taking heroin as well as pain reduction, both effects coming from the action at the opioid receptors. The 'rush' includes a dry mouth, heavy limbs, flushing of the skin, nausea and possibly itching. There is also a slowing of mental functioning, breathing and heart rate. Long-term effects include psychological and physical dependence, tolerance and cravings for the drug. If the drug is not taken, withdrawal symptoms will be experienced. Tolerance, psychological and physical dependence and withdrawal are explained below. Psychological effects include difficulties with concentration, memory and attention.

Tolerance

Tolerance (a key term) refers to the situation when more of a drug has to be taken to maintain the same effects (the term can be used with regard to any drug when this is the case). The same dose of drug will not produce the feelings of euphoria so more and more must be taken, up to a certain level. After that level it is likely that no amount of the drug will produce the feelings of euphoria and the individual continues to take the drug to prevent withdrawal symptoms. At this stage, the person is addicted and needs the drug for normal functioning but is not getting any pleasure from it.

Physical and psychological dependence

Physical dependence (a key term) is the situation when someone needs increasingly high doses to get the high they crave and so has to keep taking the drug because of this desire. The body becomes used to functioning with the drug and needs it for normal functioning — at this stage the person is physically dependent on the drug. Addiction is this situation where the body needs the drug for normal physical and/or psychological functioning. Physical dependence also means that if someone stops taking the drug, there will be withdrawal symptoms. Heroin rapidly leads to tolerance, so someone can quickly become physically dependent on it.

Psychological dependence (a key term) is the situation when the drug is important for someone's mental state, for example because it replaces social support in their lives or makes them feel better when they have problems such as unemployment or low self-esteem. In such circumstances, a person may seek to dull the senses and feel pleasure by taking the drug.

Withdrawal

Withdrawal (a key term) is the process which occurs when a person stops taking an addictive drug, often involving unpleasant physical symptoms. With heroin, withdrawal symptoms can occur even if it has only been taken for a very short time. They may start about 6 hours after stopping the drug, although the timing depends on the level of tolerance that has been reached. Symptoms include cramps, anxiety, depression, sweating, insomnia and muscle aching. There might be compulsive scratching and nausea. Taking heroin again makes the symptoms disappear.

> ### Tip
> Tolerance, physical dependence, psychological dependence and withdrawal are all key terms, defined in this section. Make sure you can define each of them and give an example in each case (e.g. with regard to heroin).

Nicotine (smoking)

This section looks at nicotine, specifically its mode of action and effects, and how tolerance, dependence and withdrawal work with regard to nicotine and smoking.

Mode of action

- Nicotine affects both the central and the peripheral nervous system and is very addictive.
- Nicotine affects the brain; it also affects other areas of the body, but it reaches the brain first.
- Nicotine works at the nicotinic receptors and inhibits (hinders) the function of specific acetylcholine receptors. Acetylcholine is a neurotransmitter.
- Nicotine stimulates the acetylcholine receptors, then blocks them, which gets in the way of normal signalling.
- Acetylcholine levels rise and this brings high levels of noradrenaline, which leads to better memory.
- There are higher levels of endorphins, which lowers anxiety.

Effects

Nicotine poisoning includes a burning feeling in the mouth, more salivation, sickness, headaches and stomach pains. The person feels agitated, confused and weak. The heart can be affected and blood pressure rises. However, smoking does not give enough nicotine for it to be directly toxic, and a low dose can improve relaxation and attention and cause mild euphoria rather than poisoning. Dopamine levels rise with nicotine, which brings heightened pleasure, as with heroin. One problem is that the lungs become coated in tar, which reduces their efficiency, and also parts of the plant (tobacco) are carcinogenic (lead to cancer).

Tolerance

Nicotine, like heroin, quickly leads to tolerance, which means that more cigarettes are smoked to get the same effect — until smoking more does not make a difference, which is when there is physical dependence. That is to say, more cigarettes will at first improve the pleasure feelings, but this only lasts a short time before a plateau is reached, and then smoking more will not change the reaction to nicotine. This means that smokers often stay at a high level of nicotine intake; they become addicted.

Physical and psychological dependence

There is rapid physical dependence because tolerance is quickly reached. The brain is changed by nicotine so that it is needed to maintain normal functioning, which is a definition of dependence. Psychological dependence is quickly reached as well. Smoking gives oral stimulation that would need to be replaced, for example, so someone who gives up smoking might eat more. Nicotine is a stimulant that leads to craving, which has a psychological element as well as a physical one. If smoking makes someone calmer, which is a desired effect, then this is rewarding, so people might continue smoking to get the reward — this involves the principles of operant conditioning.

Withdrawal

Nicotine withdrawal symptoms include a desire to eat or get oral gratification, which is missing without smoking. There can be anxiety, poor concentration and memory problems, as well as depression, sleeping problems and headaches.

Two ways of treating substance misuse

This section looks at using drug treatments for heroin and using token economy to help stop substance misuse.

Tip

If you studied a different treatment from token economy, you may prefer to revise that rather than learn about a new one.

Drug treatment for heroin addiction

Drug treatment is a major way of treating heroin addiction. Blättler et al. (2002) (pp. 34–35) looked at the use of drug treatment with heroin addicts, in order to see if it also works to reduce cocaine use in those being treated for heroin. They found that such a programme can be effective.

Drug treatment involves prescribing heroin or a substitute such as methadone. Methadone is a synthetic opiate that blocks the effects of heroin and takes away withdrawal symptoms. The treatment is offered because someone can then give up heroin without withdrawal symptoms, which often are the reason that giving up is hard. The idea is that a heroin substitute is prescribed that has different properties but will help the individual not to take heroin. Such treatments are called 'mainte- nance programmes' because they are a way of controlling heroin addiction.

Methadone is taken orally and stops withdrawal symptoms for about 24 hours, so a dose a day is required. If someone taking methadone then takes heroin, they will not get the feeling of euphoria, and that helps them to stop taking heroin. Methadone can create overdose problems, and also coming off methadone can give withdrawal symptoms.

Buprenorphine is another drug that is used to help heroin addicts and is an alterna- tive to methadone. It gives weaker opiate levels and is less likely to lead to overdose than methadone. There is also less physical dependence than with methadone.

Evaluation
Strengths
- There is evidence suggesting that maintenance programmes work, for example from Blättler et al. (2002).
- Wodak (2005) reviewed studies and found that individuals tended to continue with drug treatment programmes more often than with other treatment programmes.
- The National Institute of Health (1997) found that methadone maintenance treat- ment is effective in reducing heroin use and helps in lowering crime rates and reducing the spread of HIV/AIDS.

Weaknesses
- It is reported that 85% of patients stay on methadone for 12 months, and the treat- ment can last for 2 years, so there are cost implications.
- It is hard to evaluate the treatment, as it is not ethical to have a control group that does not get the treatment.
- Programmes are highly regulated by the government so running them is difficult.

Token economy for drug use
Token economy programmes (TEP) work on operant conditioning principles, whereby behaviour is said to be repeated if rewarded and not repeated if ignored or punished. Rewards can take the form of positive or negative reinforcement. The idea is that substance misuse is maladaptive for the individual and needs to be changed.

Token economy may be used with regard to behaviour associated with substance misuse as well as taking the drug itself. The aim is to replace the behaviour with more appropriate behaviour. That more appropriate behaviour is identified, and might involve, for example, keeping appointments when on a methadone programme, attending counselling if that is deemed to be appropriate, or stopping taking the drug (e.g. stopping smoking). Once the required behaviour is identified, instances of it are rewarded. The individual is given tokens for this approved behaviour and the tokens can be exchanged for something desirable, such as visits or television watching.

The tokens are positive reinforcers — though it is not the tokens themselves that are reinforcing, but what they buy. Punishing the maladaptive behaviour can also be part of the programme. Alternatively, **negative reinforcement** can be used to stop the unwanted behaviour; for example, privileges can be removed if that behaviour is displayed.

Steps within token economy

- Clearly identify what will be given as tokens.
- Identify what the tokens will buy.
- Identify what behaviour will be rewarded.
- Decide when tokens can be exchanged.
- Apply the programme consistently.
- Put together a programme so that shaping can take place (such as cutting down smoking, then giving up).

Contingency management therapy

A TEP in current use is contingency management therapy, which involves a voucher system where points can be earned if someone tests negative for drugs. Items that the points buy are those that encourage healthy living (the idea being to give rewards that further promote healthy behaviour). This type of therapy is part of a rehabilitation programme that discourages drug misuse and also encourages healthy living.

Evaluation

Strengths

- Studies show that such programmes work in institutions: for example, Pierce et al. (2006) showed that continuous abstinence from drug use was twice as likely for a group that had the chance to win prizes and get a reward as for the control group that had no such reward. The study was carried out with participants on a methadone treatment programme, and it was concluded that the programme and the reward system worked together to achieve greater success.
- A TEP is ethical, in that it can suit everyone and is non-invasive and overt.

Weaknesses

- Staff must consistently reinforce required behaviour, and with different staff this consistency may not be as easy as it seems to achieve. Such a programme can be time-consuming and impractical.
- Other drug users and peer group members also reinforce behaviour, and the behaviour they reinforce is likely to be different from that required by staff.
- Such a programme can neglect the rights of the individual because staff and others have control.

Tip

TEPs use learning theory principles and are within the learning approach. The programme is a contribution of the approach to society — in this case to treating drug misuse. Token economy is also used in criminological psychology. You can choose TEP when you are asked for a therapy or treatment from the learning approach in clinical psychology, and you need to know about TEP when you look at social control for the section on issues and debates (Unit 4).

Campaigns against the use of recreational drugs

This section focuses on an anti-smoking campaign. This is chosen because nicotine is selected as the 'other drug' for study in this book.

> **Tip**
>
> If you studied a different campaign you may prefer to revise that rather than learn about a new one.

Laws restricting smoking have been passed: in England in 2007 smoking was banned in any public place, following similar legislation in many European countries. Cigarette advertising is banned and there are strong warnings on cigarette packets, so it is clear that there is government backing for anti-smoking campaigns.

One specific anti-smoking campaign

In 2008, the British Heart Foundation (BHF) campaigned against smoking in what they called a 'hard-hitting' campaign. They used strong images on posters and in television advertisements to shock people into quitting. They claimed that 'stopping smoking is the single most important thing a person can do to avoid a heart attack'.

The campaign provided information about support groups and replacement therapy, such as nicotine patches. The BHF website gave information on the nearest support group and allowed people to share experiences with others as support. There was also information about the effects of smoking. For example, the site emphasised how smoking cigarettes builds up fat on artery walls and a clot can then block an artery, causing a heart attack. There was also the positive message that stopping smoking reduces the likelihood of heart problems.

Evaluation of anti-drug campaigns

Strengths

- The BHF campaign used many different media (television advertising, posters, leaflets and the website) to reach as many people as possible, and used frequent repetition to catch people's attention.
- Mechanic et al. (2005) found that in the USA smoking had fallen by half because of anti-smoking campaigns.
- Hafsted et al. (1997) used a questionnaire to evaluate reactions to Norwegian media campaigns against smoking. They found that smokers reacted more emotionally than non-smokers, and women reacted more strongly than men. Those who reacted positively were more likely to give up smoking.

Weaknesses

- The BHF campaign focusing mainly on website information will suit those who have access to the internet only — and who access the site. They may already be thinking about giving up and, although that is valuable, the campaign may not be as suitable for those not thinking about giving up.
- One campaign often has other policies and practices alongside it, such as in this case the government ban on smoking, so it is hard to say how far one campaign is successful.

Studies in detail

Blättler et al. (2002) and Ennett et al. (1994) are the two studies chosen in this book.

Tip

You may have covered a different study in detail alongside Blättler et al. (2002), and you may prefer to revise that one instead of learning a new one.

Blättler et al. (2002)

Aim(s)

- This study looked at heroin addicts on a maintenance programme who also used cocaine, and the aim was to see if the drug treatment programme would work to reduce cocaine use (as well as heroin use) in these poly-drug users.
- Specifically, the researchers asked whether there was a reduction in cocaine use among those who remained on the programme for 18 months, and what factors were associated with continued cocaine use.

Procedure

- The study involved the Medical Prescription of Narcotics Programme (PROVE), which prescribes heroin for heroin users, and the participants were those on the programme. This was a Swiss study.
- Baseline measures were taken and then follow-up measures to see the effects of the programme.
- This was a cohort study in a naturalistic setting — it was a longitudinal study following one cohort through the programme.
- Ethical approval was given and there was a group monitoring the medical therapy.
- Interviewing was carried out up to 18 months into the programme, every 6 months, using standardised questionnaires with trained interviewers.
- Some clinical measures were also taken, such as tests for drugs in the urine.
- The treatment included not only drug treatment but other care too, as well as mandatory counselling.

Results

Chi-squared and Spearman's tests were carried out on some of the data.

At the baseline measures, there were 266 participants (98 female, 168 male). The average age was 30 and the average duration of heroin use was 10 years. The data included the following:

- 75% preferred to inject heroin and cocaine
- 33% drank alcohol
- 23% used no cannabis
- 31% were daily cocaine users
- 54% were occasional cocaine users
- 16% were non-cocaine users

At the 18-month measures, 247 participants were followed up, and self-report data and urine analysis were used. The data included the following:

- 133 said they did not use cocaine. Of these, 127 participants tested negative for cocaine in the urine analysis, while 6 tested positive. These two groups made up 51% and 2% respectively of the total 247 participants.
- 114 said they used some cocaine (99 consuming occasionally and 15 consuming daily or nearly daily). Of the 114, 59 tested negative for cocaine in the urine analysis even though they self-reported as using cocaine, while 55 tested positive and also self-reported as using cocaine — these two groups made up 24% and 22% respectively of the total 247 participants.
- After 18 months of the treatment, cocaine use went down from 84% to 48%. The proportion of non-users went from 16% to 52%.

Conclusions

- The treatment was thought to be successful, as the non-users went from 16% to 52%.
- 75% of the participants had urine tests that were negative with regard to cocaine, which shows the success of the treatment programme.
- Cocaine use at the 18-month follow-up was linked to prostitution, illicit heroin use and contact with the drug scene, so other factors were found that were thought to affect drug use.

Tip

Use the findings of Blättler et al. (2002) when discussing the success of drug treatment programmes.

Evaluation of Blättler et al. (2002)

Strengths	Weaknesses
Sampling was careful, including checking drop-out rate and other factors.	Being on the study, and the additional attention, may have caused the change.
There was careful attention to ethics.	Generalisation is limited to Switzerland and those types of participant.
Both qualitative and quantitative data were gathered, so validity could be checked.	Self-report data may not be reliable.
The study was naturalistic, so had ecological validity.	
Many factors were checked for change over time, such as the price of cocaine, to try to ensure the treatment alone was responsible for any change.	

Ennett et al. (1994)

Aim(s)
- The study looked at adolescent smoking in relation to friendship cliques, gathering data about both.
- The aim was to see if peer group pressure is linked to smoking behaviour.

Procedure
- The study took place in the USA, using ninth-grade students. The data were collected in 1980, but the researchers claimed that smoking rates had not gone down in the USA since the time of the study, so the findings could be generalised to present-day (1994) behaviour.
- A self-administered questionnaire was used, and mothers were asked about their own level of education as well.
- 1,092 students were used across five schools and 87 friendship cliques were reported.
- A clique was defined as three or more adolescents within the same school who link to most other members of their group with regard to friendships (friendships between schools were not counted).
- A link that went one way (e.g. from person A to person B) was assumed to be a two-way friendship (a reciprocal link), but greater weight was placed on actual reciprocal links (where both mentioned the friendship).
- 42.2% of those taking part were clique members and the others were isolates or liaisons (liaisons were friends with others but not members of a clique).

Results
- 87 cliques were found and that included 461 adolescents (42%).
- 93% of cliques had between three and ten members; the average clique size was five members.
- Members of a clique were generally similar with regard to gender and race (there were very few mixed cliques).
- 89.8% of all clique members were non-smokers.
- 68% of cliques were comprised entirely of non-smokers, and 2% entirely of smokers.

Conclusions
- Clique members who smoked tended to associate with one another, but there were not many of them.
- Perhaps peer groups contribute more to not smoking than to smoking.
- Isolates had the highest level of smoking, which backs this up.
- The finding also relates to social learning theory as an explanation of substance misuse (or lack of such misuse).
- Perhaps non-smokers become cliques rather than cliques becoming non-smokers.

Evaluation of Ennett et al. (1994)

Strengths	Weaknesses
Cliques are found from analysing the data and then members of cliques themselves say whether they smoke — valid data.	Only three best friends were asked about, which might limit the data's validity.
There was thorough sampling (trying to get all ninth-graders, using five schools), so generalisation is possible up to a point.	Non-reciprocated friendships were accepted as reciprocated, whereas the friendship might not have been 'real'.
	There may have been social desirability in the responses about not smoking.
	Self-report data can be unreliable.

Evidence in practice: key issue and practical

The issues chosen here are why drug abuse should be treated and how drug abuse can be treated.

> **Tip**
>
> If you covered a different key issue you might prefer to revise that rather than learn another.

The issue of why drug abuse should be treated

Drug abuse is something that society wishes to get rid of for a number of social and economic reasons. Those who are addicted to drugs can have more health problems. Smoking cigarettes is linked with heart attacks and drinking alcohol is linked with liver problems. Renal disease is also said to link to drug misuse. Drug abuse is also linked to crime, for example when an addict needs funds for their habit. The cost to a society in economic terms, therefore, is high. In social terms, too, it is seen as desirable that drug abuse is treated because peer groups are said to affect drug misuse in that they give social support. This might be seen as a good thing, but they can also mean it is hard to give up, which might be seen as a bad thing. The issue of why drug abuse should be treated links to reasons for health campaigns and promoting good health.

The issue of how drug abuse can be treated

There are different treatments for drug abuse and some rest on the medical model of illness, which would suggest that biological measures will work when treating biological problems. Another model that treatments rest on is the social learning model, which suggests that substance misuse comes from observational learning, so treatments might rely on observational learning as well. If it is thought that drug taking is linked to genes and inherited characteristics, then this is about nature and a biological remedy might be preferred. However, if it is thought that drug taking is linked to learned behaviour, then this is about nurture, and changing the environment or experiences in some way might be seen as an appropriate way to treat substance misuse.

> **Tip**
>
> The description above nearly moves into theory, but not quite. It is advisable to keep theory for the explanation of the issue.

Ideas and concepts from health psychology about treatment for drug misuse

Two treatments for drug abuse have been covered in the content section (pp. 30–32), so you can use that material here. Drug treatment programmes are used and have been shown to be successful (e.g. Blättler et al. 2002), although they often involve counselling and other support such as help with debt management, so it might not be just the maintenance drug treatment that brings about any success. Token economy has been used, based on operant conditioning principles, and has also been shown to have some success. Evaluations of the two treatment programmes show their relative merits and disadvantages (pp. 31–32).

Practical

The practical suggested for this health psychology section is an analysis of two article sources, where a summary of the two articles is put together and then concepts and ideas from the application used to explain the articles. The articles have to be about the material in your course in health psychology, and it makes sense to use articles about the key issue you have chosen — in this case how drug abuse can be treated.

The internet has many articles on drug treatment and its effectiveness, and a good place to start would be official health websites such as the NHS website. Drug rehabilitation centres have websites that give information, and there are special programmes, such as the 12-step treatment programme. These sites will give articles that you can use, or you can use newspaper articles or journal articles.

Summarise each article, showing what it is about. Put together the two summaries so that you are describing the material. Then bring in concepts and ideas from health psychology to explain the overall summary or to add information as appropriate.

Sport psychology
Summary of what you need to know

> **Tip**
>
> In this study guide, choices are made for you, to limit the material. However, if you have studied a different choice it is probably better to revise that, rather than learn something new at this stage.

Definition of the application

You need to be able to:

- define sport psychology in terms of what is involved in the application, including how people choose certain sports, what makes someone good at sport, and other issues, such as how to improve sporting performance
- define key terms, including participation, excellence, intrinsic motivation, extrinsic motivation, arousal, anxiety, audience effect, qualitative data, quantitative data

Methodology and how science works

You need to be able to:

- describe and evaluate the use of questionnaires and correlations in sport psychology
- consider, when evaluating these two methods, their use in sport psychology and reliability, validity and ethical issues
- outline what is meant by both qualitative and quantitative data and compare them in terms of strengths and weaknesses

Content

You need to be able to do the following.

- Describe and evaluate personality traits as an explanation for individual differences in sporting participation and performance.
- Describe and evaluate one other explanation for individual differences in sporting participation and performance. In this book the other explanation is the effect of socialisation.
- Describe and evaluate the achievement motivation theory and one other theory of motivation. In this book the other theory is self-efficacy.
- Describe and evaluate the inverted U hypothesis and one other theory about the effects of arousal/anxiety or the audience. In this book the other theory is evaluation apprehension theory.
- Describe and evaluate two psychological techniques for improving performance in sport. In this book the techniques are imagery and goal-setting.

Studies in detail

You need to learn two studies in detail. The main one for sport psychology is Boyd and Munroe's (2003) study of the use of imagery in climbers and in track and field athletes. The other study has to be one from Cottrell et al. (1968), Koivula (1995) and Craft et al. (2003). In this book all three are referred to, but Koivula is the one discussed in detail.

Evidence in practice: key issue and practical

You need to be able to describe one key issue from the application. In this guide, the chosen issue is gender differences in sporting participation. You also need to carry out a practical based on the material in the course. In this guide, the practical is a content analysis based on the key issue of gender differences in sporting participation.

Definition of the application

This section looks at what sport psychology is about and at some of the key terms.

A good way of extending a definition, when 3 marks are available, is to add an example.

Sport psychology is about the sports people choose (participation), how well they do (performance) and how to improve sporting performance. The focus on coaching and how to improve includes looking at motivation, goal-setting and imagery. Sport psychology offers explanations for participation choices and for performance levels. Explanations include theories about the effects of motivation, arousal, anxiety and other factors, such as the presence of an audience and whether the audience is just there or is evaluating performance. In most applications in psychology there is focus on explanations, theory and then treatments. In sport psychology there is focus on explanations, theory and then how to improve performance — which is not quite the same as looking at treatments but is still about applying theory. There is also focus on excellence and how to achieve it.

Key terms

The key terms are only briefly defined here; more detailed explanations of most are given in the methodology and content sections.

- **Participation** concerns which sport someone chooses to take part in. Issues here include whether participation is affected by personality traits (e.g. introverts might prefer individual to group sport) and/or by gender.
- **Excellence** involves doing something extremely well, as with performers who are at the top of their sport and become champions. There is great interest in excellence because it is a goal of many sportspeople.

- **Intrinsic motivation** (p. 58) is motivation driven by internal factors, for example the desire to win coming from a need to achieve well.
- **Extrinsic motivation** (p. 58) is motivation driven by external factors, for example the desire to win being driven by prize money.
- **Arousal** (p. 61) refers to a biological state of alertness, in which, for example, the heart beats faster, and pulse rate and breathing rate are high.
- **Anxiety** (p. 62) is a state that includes arousal as well as worrying thoughts.
- The **audience effect** (p. 62) refers to the effect on performance of having someone watching (and possibly evaluating performance rather than just being there).
- **Qualitative data** (p. 52) are data that are rich in detail and collected using methods such as open questioning.
- **Quantitative data** (p. 52) are data that are in number format, such as percentages or numbers in a rating scale.

> **Tip**
> Use the key terms in a definition of sport psychology, for example suggesting that factors of interest include arousal and anxiety.

Methodology and how science works

This section looks at questionnaires and correlations, giving description and evaluation of both these methods. There is also focus on qualitative and quantitative data, including comparison of these two kinds of data.

> **Tip**
> Use your AS learning about questionnaires, including qualitative and quantitative data (in the social approach). Also use your understanding of correlations from the psychodynamic approach.

Questionnaires

This section describes and evaluates the use of questionnaires in general and in sport psychology in particular.

Description of questionnaires in general
- Questionnaires often use both closed and open questions.
- Closed questions gather quantitative data and give the respondent a choice of answers from which they must chose their response(s).
- Open questions gather qualitative data and leave the respondent space to give their attitudes, opinions or more detail in their answer.
- Questionnaires often use Likert-type questions, which means the respondent ticks from a choice such as 'strongly agree', 'agree', 'unsure', 'disagree' and 'strongly disagree', though in fact Likert-type questions often use a 7-point scale instead of a 5-point scale.

- Koivula (1995) uses Likert-type questions when looking at how sports can be gendered (allocated to male, female or neutral according to who participates) and at how people gender themselves (sex-typed or not). Koivula's study is explained in detail below (pp. 44–46).

Use of questionnaires in sport psychology

Two of the studies in detail for this application use questionnaires. One is the Boyd and Munroe (2003) study that is compulsory and the other is Koivula's (1995) study. Both these studies are explained in detail here so that you can use them as examples of using questionnaires in sport psychology. This detail needs to be learned so that you have covered the required two studies in detail for this application.

Boyd and Munroe (2003)

Boyd and Munroe (2003) carried out a study in Canada which looked at the use of imagery of different types in sport. The following table presents important background information for their study. It sets out five different functions of imagery with explanations and examples — showing, for instance, that cognitive specific imagery helps to improve specific skills, such as a tennis serve.

The five functions of imagery

Imagery function	Explanation	Example
Cognitive specific (CS)	Learn specific skill	Tennis serve
Cognitive general (CG)	Learn a strategy	Dance routine
Motivational general-mastery (MG-M)	Learn self-confidence, belief in ability	Control when referee makes a poor decision
Motivational general-arousal (MG-A)	Learn to control anxiety and arousal	Not being anxious when performing
Motivational specific (MS)	Learn to focus on goals such as a championship	Keep motivated when training, even if no immediate reward is in sight

Aim(s)

- to compare track and field athletes with climbers to see if their use of imagery differs because of the differences in the requirements of the sports
- to compare beginner and expert climbers with regard to their use of imagery
- to study the use of imagery in sport, including different types of cognitive and motivational imagery

Hypotheses

There were two main hypotheses. One hypothesis was that climbers would differ from track and field athletes in the five functions of imagery. Within this hypothesis, the following more specific predictions were made:

- Climbers would use CG strategy for route finding.
- Climbers would use CG more than track and field athletes.
- Climbers would use MG-A extensively to control fear and anxiety.
- Climbers would rate low on use of MS (which focuses on extrinsic motivation) compared to track and field athletes.

The second main hypothesis was that beginner and expert climbers would differ in the five functions of imagery, with more specific predictions as follows:

- Beginners would use more MG-A because they may be more fearful.
- Advanced climbers would use more CG because they climb more difficult routes.

Procedure

- Participants included 38 track and field athletes (13 females and 25 males) from a university track and field team. There were 48 climbers (28 males and 20 females) from two different climbing groups in Canada.
- The Sport Imagery Questionnaire (SIQ) was used with the track and field athletes, and a modified version of it was used with the climbers (CIQ). The SIQ asks about 'competing', so the climbers were given a modified version which asked about 'climbing' instead.
- The SIQ has 30 items and measures the frequency of imagery on the five subscales using a 7-point Likert scale (1 = rarely and 7 = very often).
- There was a 91% return rate for the track and field athletes and a 100% return rate for the climbers.
- Climbers were asked about their hardest climb and then rated as beginner or advanced accordingly.

Results

- There were no significant gender differences found.
- Track and field athletes had a higher mean score on the MS subscale, which was about focusing on winning and rewards.
- Climbers had a lower mean score on the MG-M subscale, which was about being mentally tough.
- Track and field athletes had a higher MG-A score (learning to reduce fear and arousal) than the climbers.
- There was no significant difference between beginner climbers and advanced climbers (see table).

The mean score of beginners and advanced climbers on the five subscales

	Beginner climbers	Advanced climbers
CS	4.26	4.71
CG	4.31	4.90
MS	3.22	2.79
MG-M	4.47	4.73
MG-A	4.03	4.40

Conclusions

- One hypothesis suggested that climbers would use CG and MG-A extensively and MS less often, and the finding that climbers had a lower score on MS, MG-A and MG-M partly supports this hypothesis (though they were lower on MG-A than was thought). Climbers focus on reward less and also focus less on learning to be tough and boosting self-confidence.
- MG-A was lower for climbers than was expected. This may have been because the track and field athletes were asked about competitions so may have focused more on a recent competition. On the other hand, climbers were asked about climbing so may have focused less on actual competitions.
- Perhaps the reason that beginner and advanced climbers were not significantly different with regard to MG-A was that advanced climbers were focusing on more difficult climbs so their anxiety levels were relatively similar.

Evaluation of Boyd and Munroe (2003)

Strengths	Weaknesses
A standardised questionnaire was used, giving some consistency and reliability.	There was a small sample and only climbers climbing indoors were used, so bias in sampling may make generalising hard.
The study used the same procedures and questions in the main, so it had good controls.	The two questionnaires differed, so comparing them may not be valid.
	Assignment to beginner or advanced for each climber was by self-report, which may not be reliable, and the decision about where to cut the climb rating was sudden.
	One group did the survey together and the others completed it independently.

Koivula (1995)

Koivula looked at how views about gender might affect views about sport with regard to the gender of participants.

Aims

- to look at how people see the world by processing information using schemas gained through development, and how gender affects such schemas (this is called gender-based schematic information processing)
- to see whether people who have strongly gender-based schemas are more likely to see sports as 'male' or 'female' than those with less strongly gender-based schemas (those with strongly gender-based schemas are called 'sex-typed')
- to look at the effects of gender on the ratings of particular sports depending on whether the person rating is male or female

Procedure

The study was done in Sweden, with 104 females and 103 males taking part. Two questionnaires were used.

One questionnaire was the Bem Sex Role Inventory (BSRI). This uses 60 personality traits and respondents are asked to rate themselves on each trait on a 7-point scale from 'never/almost never true' to 'always/almost always true'. There are 20 'masculine traits', 20 'feminine' traits, and 20 other items, so that not all items are about masculinity or femininity. From the BSRI score each participant is given a masculinity/femininity score and each is classified as sex-typed (matching the characteristics of their gender), cross sex-typed (having the opposite characteristics from their gender), androgynous (in the middle of the two gender types) or undifferentiated (none of the other three). The BSRI gave eight groups, one each for the four types for each gender.

The other questionnaire asked about the appropriateness of males or females participating in certain sports. Again a 7-point scale was used, with 'very appropriate to men and not at all for women' at one end of the scale and 'very appropriate to women and not at all for men' at the other end of the scale. A rating of 4 meant 'equally appropriate for both men and women'. Then sports were rated as 'male', 'female' or 'neutral' according to the average. A score of 1–3.5 gave a 'male' sport, a score of 4 gave a 'neutral' sport and a score of 4.5–7 gave a 'female' sport. There were 34 'neutral' sports, 18 'masculine' sports and seven 'feminine' sports. Feminine sports were, for example, aerobics, dance and ballet. Masculine sports included baseball, boxing and football.

Koivula then looked to see if strongly sex-typed individuals would rate sports as either 'male' or 'female', whereas androgynous individuals would not use gender schemas as much and would more often rate sports as 'neutral'. So she compared their type (sex-typed, cross sex-typed, androgynous or undifferentiated) with their average score for allocating gender to sports.

Results

- The BSRI found 'sex-typed' to be the largest group for both males and females.
- Most sports were rated as neutral (34, as against 18 rated as male and seven as female).
- Androgynous women rated the gender appropriateness of sports as close to 'equally appropriate' (using an average rating), as expected.
- In general, participants agreed on the ratings of the different sports as 'male', 'female' or 'neutral'.
- The eight BSRI groups differed on their ratings of the three sport types ('male', 'female' or 'neutral').
- Age did not correlate with the BSRI scores or with sports ratings.

Conclusions

- Sports are affected by gender labelling.
- People are fairly consistent in deciding which sports are appropriate to males, females or both.

- In general people are sex-typed, which means they use gender-based schematic processing.
- Possibly men use gender stereotyping more than women, and androgynous or undifferentiated types do not in general use gender-based schematic processing.
- Perhaps male domination in society is validated by sport and physical activities, and boys model on fathers who display gender-appropriate characteristics.

Evaluation of Koivula (1995)

Strengths	Weaknesses
Participants decide if a sport is male, female or neutral, so there is some validity in the categorisation.	There might be a problem in generalising results from Swedish society and culture.
The BSRI has 20 filler items to avoid demand characteristics.	Self-ratings might lack reliability.
	Asking about gender to test gender might mean findings are biased by demand characteristics and are not valid.
	The sample is restricted (mainly young white students), so generalising may be difficult.

Evaluation of use of questionnaires in sport psychology

To an extent you can use the evaluations of Boyd and Munroe (2003) and Koivula (1995) to evaluate the use of questionnaires in sport.

Keeping the procedure the same

It is necessary to keep the procedure exactly the same when gathering data using questionnaires. For example, when Boyd and Munroe (2003) used a slightly different questionnaire with the climbers than with the track and field athletes, this was said to have possibly affected the findings, as the track and field athletes were asked about competing whereas the climbers were asked about climbing. This could have affected whether the comparisons between the two were fair.

Using rating scales

It might be that rating scales are interpreted differently by different respondents. One person's idea of 'rarely', for example, might be different from someone else's inter-pretation so the data might not be properly comparable. The data might not be reliable either — if the scales were interpreted differently, then the findings might differ if the study were to be repeated.

Validity

It might not be valid to say that a rating score, for example, given for a characteristic that might apply to you, is a real measure. You might answer differently on a different day, which would affect reliability; or you might answer as you think you should, which would involve demand characteristics and would not give valid data. Social desirability could affect answers as well, for example in Koivula's (1995) study, where people might have guessed what 'should' be thought of as 'masculine' sports.

Standardisation of questionnaires

The BSRI is a standardised questionnaire, in that it has been used in more than one study and found to measure what is being asked about. The SIQ is also a standardised questionnaire. Studies in sport psychology can use standardised questionnaires rather than specially developed ones and this can add to both the validity and the reliability of the data. Using the same questionnaire can also make data comparable within and between the studies. Craft et al. (2003) carried out a meta-analysis of studies that had all used the same questionnaire (the CSAI-2). As the studies used the same tool, their findings could be reliably compared.

Measuring attitudes or personality

Sport psychology often measures attitudes to sport, or aspects of personality that link to sport. For example, participation, performance, motivation and excellence all involve attitudes and personality, as well as other internal factors, such as intrinsic motivation. Questionnaires are useful in measuring such internal factors, because they use self-report data, which asks people about themselves.

Evaluation of the questionnaire as a research method

Questionnaires can be evaluated in terms of validity, reliability and ethics.

Reliability

Strengths

- The reliability of data from questionnaires can be checked using split-half reliability. This means using items from the questionnaire that ask for the same data and splitting them into two halves. Then each person's score on one half can be correlated with their score on the other half. If the two halves 'match' with regard to scores, then the questionnaire is reliable.
- Pilot studies can check that items are clearly understood. If questions are clearly understood then the data are more likely to be consistent, which makes them reliable.

Weaknesses

- On one day people might give different answers from on another day, according to their mood or what is happening to them at the time, for example.
- Demand characteristics can affect reliability as well as validity, as one researcher might elicit a different response from another researcher, perhaps by their dress or manner.

Validity

Strengths

- When qualitative data are collected using open questions, questionnaires can be said to be valid — the data is in-depth and has detail, so 'real-life' data are more likely to be gathered than when data are quantitative (e.g. when rating scales are used).

- Validity can be claimed when different questions cover the same area so can be checked for agreement. If they agree then there is validity.

Weaknesses
- Even the open questions can give limited data, as they are usually restricted to a short answer that cannot easily be elaborated upon.
- Answers may be affected by social desirability, when a respondent answers as they think they should. This would mean that answers lack validity.

Ethics
Strengths
- There can be clear instructions on a questionnaire that give the right to withdraw, and detail about the aims and objectives of the study. Informed consent can be gained by assuming that those who fill in the questionnaire have agreed to it.
- Questionnaires can demonstrate anonymity and confidentiality, because they can avoid asking for any personal information and the respondent will know that this information has not been given.

Weaknesses
- Even though instructions can be quite detailed, often full information is not given in order to avoid demand characteristics. For example, the BSRI has 20 filler items to avoid too much emphasis on male and female characteristics.
- With postal questionnaires, there is a limit to how much information can be given (e.g. on the purpose of the study or how the findings will be used), because all instructions will be written and it cannot be assumed that respondents will read the information and understand what the study is about.

Correlations

This section looks at description and evaluation of the correlational method, as well as giving examples of correlations in sport psychology and evaluation of how correlations are used in sport psychology.

Tip

When answering questions within an application about methodology, be ready to discuss the methodology as it is used in that application, as well as the methodology in general.

Description of the correlational method in general
- Correlations are more a matter of design than a research method, as different research methods (such as interviews and questionnaires) can generate correlational data.
- Koivula (1995) used correlations to look at age and rating of sports as 'male', 'female' or 'neutral'.
- When one person has two scores on any variables, then a correlational test can be carried out. This is done by gathering the scores on the two variables for a number of participants and then carrying out a correlational test, such as Spearman's.

- If as one score rises the other rises too, this is a positive correlation. For example, suppose that, as age rises, the average rating score for sport as gendered rises. This would suggest a positive relationship between age and using gender schemas with regard to sports — that is, the older people are, the more they use gender stereotyping.
- If as one score rises the other falls, this is a negative correlation. For example, suppose that, as age rises, the average rating score for sport as gendered falls. This would suggest a negative relationship between age and using gender schemas with regard to sport — that is, the older people are, the less they use gender stereotyping with regard to sport.
- A correlation (the result from a statistical test) that is near +1 is a positive correlation, a correlation that is near −1 is a negative correlation and a score near 0 means there is no correlation.
- +0.68 is likely to be a high positive correlation and +0.38 is less likely to be significant, though the test has to be carried out to find significance as factors like number of participants make a difference. +0.68 is a stronger correlation than +0.38.
- A correlation can be weak (e.g. −0.32) but significant.

Correlations in sport psychology

An example of the use of correlation in sport psychology is Craft et al. (2003), a study that is listed in the optional studies in detail for your course. The study is only briefly outlined here, but you could find out more and use the study as one of the studies in detail. Koivula (1995) also used correlational analysis, as discussed below.

Koivula (1995)

Koivula (1995) used correlational analysis to test for relationships between age and BSRI gender classification, and between age and 'gendering' of sports. This was not explained above when her study was discussed in detail (pp. 44–46), because it was a small part of the study and there were no significant findings with regard to age (no relationships were found). She asked respondents to give their age as part of the questionnaires she administered and then she used their scores on the rating scales to carry out correlational tests. Evaluation of Koivula (1995) is given earlier in this section (p. 46).

Craft et al. (2003)

Craft et al. (2003) carried out a meta-analysis of 29 studies that looked for a relationship between anxiety and sports performance. All the studies had used the CSAI-2 (Competitive State Anxiety Inventory), which gives scores for cognitive anxiety, somatic anxiety and self-confidence. Cognitive anxiety is the psychological side of anxiety and somatic anxiety is the physical side. Because all the studies had used the same inventory, Craft et al. (2003) could use correlational statistical tests to see which factors linked with the three elements (cognitive and somatic anxiety, and self-confidence) and to see how they related to one another. Overall, the study found that self-confidence relates to sporting performance. The more self-confident someone is, the better they perform. The study also showed that cognitive and somatic anxiety relate to one another.

The relationship strength between cognitive anxiety, somatic anxiety and self-confidence

Type of anxiety as measured by CSAI-2	Result of correlational test
Cognitive anxiety related to somatic anxiety	$r = 0.52$
Cognitive anxiety related to self-confidence	$r = -0.47$
Somatic anxiety related to self-confidence	$r = -0.54$

All three results are strong enough to be significant. Note that the first one is a positive correlation, which means as cognitive anxiety rises, so does somatic anxiety. The last two are negative correlations — as self-confidence rises cognitive anxiety falls, as does somatic anxiety. These results are what would be expected, given our understanding of what anxiety and self-confidence are. Self-confidence can be seen as the opposite of anxiety.

Evaluation of Craft et al. (2003)

Strengths

- Comparisons could be made as the studies in the meta-analysis used the same questionnaire.
- There was a large sample because of the large number of studies, so generalisation was possible, as findings were similar between the studies.

Weaknesses

- Craft et al. (2003) point out that the relationship between cognitive anxiety and performance was not straightforward and other variables had to be taken into account. It is possible that the CSAI-2 is not reliable because different variables may have affected the results in the different studies.
- A questionnaire can only measure part of performance. (As well as self-report data, other factors were also found to be important, including type of sport, type of athlete, and time the questionnaire was administered.) Therefore, conclusions about performance from self-report data might not be valid, as they are only part of the situation.

Evaluation of correlations

The course asks you to be able to evaluate correlations in terms of validity, reliability and ethics, as well as in terms of how they are used in sport psychology.

Reliability

Strengths

- Correlational analysis involves a statistical technique on sets of data so is easy to repeat. This means that findings can be tested for reliability.
- Correlational data are often collected using questionnaires, which are also quite easily repeated because they are written out and in a set format. Reliable data are therefore likely to be obtained.

Weaknesses

- Correlational data are often obtained using surveys and in particular, questionnaires, and self-report data tends to lack reliability because people's answers may vary from day to day — for example, they may answer differently depending on their mood, or, with regard to sport, depending on whether they have just done well or done badly.

● Demand characteristics can affect reliability — a different researcher on a different day might elicit different responses, perhaps because of their dress or manner.

Validity

Strengths

● Correlational data is often valid because it is about real-life variables, such as age or the number of times someone has won.

● Correlations do not claim to show anything other than a relationship between two variables so there is validity in the claim that the variables co-vary. There is no claim that one affects the other in any causal way.

Weaknesses

● Demand characteristics can affect self-report data. For example, although scores like age are unlikely to be affected (unless someone lies about their age), other scores such as ratings of attitudes or feelings may vary according to what someone thinks is wanted. So the data can lack validity.

● Social desirability can affect the validity of the findings, because someone might say what they think they ought to say in terms of abiding by social norms.

Ethics

Strengths

● Correlational analysis is statistical analysis and unlikely to cause distress — there is often no manipulation of variables as in an experiment and no invasion, as in some biological measures.

● Confidentiality and privacy can usually be maintained, as the analysis involves people as numbers rather than as individuals. Correlational analysis looks at how two scores co-vary, rather than looking at specific individuals.

Weaknesses

● Findings might be detrimental to certain people (such as certain groups of sports-people) if findings from a correlational analysis show, for example, that a certain personality type will not succeed as well in a certain sport. Someone with that 'unsuitable' personality type might not be chosen for a team.

● Correlations themselves are unlikely to be unethical, but research methods used to gather the data for the correlational analysis might be unethical. For example, one of the surveys that Craft et al. (2003) used in their meta-analysis might not have been carried out ethically but this might not be known by other researchers using the data.

Evaluation of correlations as used in sport psychology

Strengths

● It is possible to build a body of knowledge because in sport psychology, standard questionnaires are often used (such as the SIQ, the BSRI and the CSAI-2), which means that comparisons can be made between the findings of different studies.

- Using a correlational technique gives figures that provide a clear picture; for example, in a table of results. For example, 0.89 is a strong correlation and 0.13 is a weak one and that would be clear to anyone looking at the findings.
- Correlations from self-report data often involve personal issues, so lend themselves well to sport psychology, which tends to focus on such issues.

Weaknesses
- A correlation just looks for a relationship between two variables, which might not be the whole picture. There may be other related variables that were not looked at.
- Correlations do not show a cause-and-effect relationship; they only show that two variables co-vary (change together).

Tip

Evaluation points can be quite hard to make clearly. It is a good idea to use examples to illustrate what is meant (as in some of the points above). This helps to show understanding and to communicate clearly and effectively. When giving examples, make sure they are within the relevant application.

Qualitative and quantitative data

You are asked to be able to show what qualitative and quantitative data are, as well as to compare them.

Qualitative data

Qualitative data (a key term) are data involving attitudes, opinions and in-depth information. For example, in a case study, a case history is often written up, and the detail and depth make the data qualitative rather than quantitative. Ways of gathering qualitative data include open questions or using a diary method or a thought record.

Qualitative data are analysed by finding themes in the data, such as the mention by all winners of reaching a 'flow' state. Themes come from the data, rather than being generated by the researcher, and then evidence for them is sought.

Quantitative data

Quantitative data (a key term) are data that are in number form. Calculations can be carried out on those numbers, even if only to say how many items or instances there are in each category that is being looked at. For example, age is quantitative, as is a number on a rating scale or a mean average. Koivula (1995) found the mean average gender rating for a sport and 'gendered' the sport accordingly. She was using quantitative data.

Quantitative data can be analysed using inferential statistics, such as Spearman's test to see how significant a correlation is.

Comparing qualitative and quantitative data

- Qualitative data involve stories, detail and depth, whereas quantitative data give no depth. Therefore qualitative data are likely to show validity, being more about 'real life'.

- Qualitative data are more useful than quantitative data when not much is known about a situation. For example, Boyd and Munroe (2003) were able to use self-report data to find out about five functions of imagery because such functions had already been researched. However, if not much was known about imagery, gathering qualitative data would be useful.
- Quantitative data are easier to analyse in some ways because tests can be done, and can be repeated over and over again. The tests are relatively quick and can be done using a computer, whereas with qualitative data, all data have to be transcribed and this can be very time-consuming and painstaking.
- Quantitative data are analysed more objectively because different people doing the tests would come up with the same results. Objectivity is important in science, so some might say that qualitative data give less scientific results — though in practice, any generating of themes from qualitative data must be done using evidence from the data.

Content

This section looks at two explanations for individual differences in participation and performance in sport; two theories of motivation; two theories of arousal, anxiety and the audience; and two psychological techniques for improving performance in sport.

Two explanations for individual differences in sporting participation and performance

In this section the effect of personality traits on sporting participation and perform-ance is discussed first. This is a biological explanation. Next the effect of socialisa-tion is discussed as the second explanation. It comes from the social approach.

> **Tip**
> If you have covered a different second explanation then you may prefer to revise that instead of learning a new one.

The effect of personality: a biological explanation

Traits are enduring characteristics that affect someone's behaviour. They are relatively stable characteristics. For example, if someone is aggressive in one situation and it is likely that they will also be aggressive in another situation, aggression would be said to be a trait for that person.

Personality traits make someone individual and such theories are said to be about individual differences — in this application, differences that affect sporting perform-ance and sporting participation. Traits might be useful for someone participating in a certain sport or they might hinder participation. They might help with regard to sporting success. Theories look at what traits go with which type of sport and what traits go with winning in certain sports.

Eysenck's (1947) theory

Eysenck (1947) put forward a model of personality, which is about types, and within his small number of types of personality there are numerous traits. In a type theory, when someone is of one type they cannot be of the opposite type. Eysenck put forward two main dimensions, each with two opposing types. One dimension is extroversion/introversion and one is neuroticism/stability. Someone cannot be both an introvert and an extrovert and they cannot be both neurotic and stable. They can be a stable introvert or a stable extrovert, however.

Introversion means focusing internally rather than on other people, and not seeking stimulation from external events. Extroversion means focusing on getting stimulation from others and from external events. Someone who is an introvert might be quiet, reserved and controlled, whereas an extrovert might be outgoing and sociable.

Neuroticism is like moodiness, where someone tends to become emotional and upset. Stability is the opposite, where someone is constant in their emotions.

Eysenck used a questionnaire with 39 items, and 700 soldiers as participants. He found that personality types could be described in terms of a dimension of introversion/extroversion and a separate dimension of stability/neuroticism. Characteristics related to introversion/extroversion did not relate at all in his analysis with characteristics related to stability/neuroticism, which is why he identified these two clear dimensions. The questionnaires used 'yes'/'no' answers to find out which personality trait applied to an individual.

Later (in 1986), the dimension of psychoticism was added. Psychoticism refers to people who find it hard to deal with reality; they may be manipulative or antisocial.

A biological explanation of extroversion/introversion (E)

Eysenck thought that personality traits are inherited. He thought that introversion/extroversion (E) is about having a balance between being stimulated and inhibited. The ascending reticular activating system (ARAS) in the brain stem works by inhibiting (damping down) or enhancing sense data to maintain an individual's emotional balance. An extrovert has a strong nervous system and the ARAS tends to inhibit it, which makes the extrovert under-aroused, so they seek excitement. An introvert has a weaker nervous system so the ARAS excites it more, and the introvert does not seek further stimulation.

A biological explanation of neuroticism/stability (N)

The neurotic/stable (N) dimension relates to the autonomic nervous system (ANS) and the limbic system. The sympathetic branch of the ANS prepares the organism for flight or fight action. This involves raised heart rate, increased breathing rate, higher blood pressure and so on (arousal is explained on p. 61). Someone high on the N scale (high on neuroticism) has an ANS that quickly produces the alarm reaction to stressful situations, whereas a more stable person reacts more slowly.

Evaluation of Eysenck's personality theory

Strengths
- It seems extroverts tire more easily (Eysenck 1967), which would fit the theory, as they would work harder to find more excitement, given their damped-down system.
- There is also evidence that introverts do better on tasks where they can concentrate for longer, which supports the theory about the ARAS.

Weaknesses
- Eysenck's questionnaire had 'yes' or 'no' answers and gave no room for any expansion, so there might be a lack of validity in the findings.
- Most testing focuses on those who are near the end of the two dimensions and little focuses on those in the middle of them.

Personality and sporting performance

Introverts need less stimulation, so should do better in sports that need precision and concentration. Extroverts seek arousal, so should do better at sports that have an audience or put the individual under pressure.

Cooper (1969) found that international athletes (who are, therefore, successful) are more competitive and outgoing than non-athletes. This fits with Eysenck's theory. Terry (2000) found that athletes who did well were less anxious and more vigorous as well as less confused and more extroverted. This, too, fits with Eysenck's theory.

Williams and Parkin (1980) found that international athletes (more successful) differed significantly in personality from club players (in hockey), which suggests that personality affects success. The study used a different personality test and theory from Eysenck, but this is still evidence that personality plays a role in sporting performance.

Personality and sporting participation

Kroll and Crenshaw (1970) found that footballers and wrestlers have similar personalities, whereas gymnasts and those doing karate had different personalities — both from each other and from footballers and wrestlers. This is evidence that personality might affect sporting choice and participation.

Skirkan (2000) found that hardiness and a sense of coherence meant that someone suffered less from stress, which suggests that personality does link with biological factors. Their findings also suggested that athletes might have the personality traits of hardiness and a sense of coherence a little more than non-athletes. Perhaps this sort of personality leads someone to choose sporting activities.

Personality might affect whether someone takes exercise, which is similar to participation in sport. Courneya and Hellsten (1998) found that personality does affect whether people exercise or not, but Mikel (1986) found that exercise affects personality. Factors like personality and sport participation go together but there may not be a causal link. Personality might affect how people feel during or after exercise (Lochbaum and Lutz 2005). Studies tend to find that extroversion links to exercise behaviour, which fits with Eysenck's theory.

Evaluation of personality theories in explaining sporting performance and participation

Strengths
- Personality tests, which tend to be questionnaires, give quantitative measures for factors like introversion, extroversion and stability, which otherwise are hard to quantify and measure. Quantitative data can be dealt with scientifically, have objectivity and are tested using statistics. They can be used when comparing studies.
- Findings about personality factors or dimensions can be applied to sport to improve performance or to help find what suits an individual, so there is a practical application to quantifying personality.

Weaknesses
- Questionnaires can limit the choice of answers and reduce validity.
- Self-report data might not be valid, as there might be demand characteristics or social desirability.
- Rather than personality affecting success in sport, it might be more that success in sport affects personality.

The effect of socialisation: a social explanation

Socialisation is about nurture, whereas according to Eysenck, personality is about nature. Studying the effect of socialisation means looking at how upbringing and environment might affect choice of sport (participation) or success in sport (performance).

Defining socialisation and social learning

Socialisation refers to how an individual learns about their culture and society. Socialising influences include family, school, peers, media and friends. Socialisation is considered a two-way process — it is not so much that someone is socialised by others as that they are active in the process of becoming socialised. For example, how someone responds to praise is specific to them and can affect how they are praised at another time.

Social learning involves learning by paying attention to a behaviour carried out by a role model, remembering the behaviour, being motivated to reproduce the behaviour and then imitating it. Vicarious learning is learning by watching others being reinforced or punished for a particular behaviour, which then affects the person's own behaviour. Operant conditioning is also involved in socialisation, when someone repeats behaviour they are rewarded for and does not repeat behaviour they are punished for.

Socialisation and sporting participation

Studies suggest that socialisation in a family affects an individual's schemata, which are ways of looking at the world. For example, gender-based schemata seem to be used to judge whether a sport is 'male', 'neutral' or 'female' (Koivula 1995). If individuals see certain sports as more suitable for them than others, this will affect which sports they participate in.

Schools encourage certain types of sporting behaviour and this, too, is said to be part of socialisation and is likely to guide choice of sport. The media also influence social-isation by making choices about which sport they show and about other aspects of the sport shown, such as male or female participation. For example, the media focus on male football, rugby and cricket, although females do take part in those sports.

It seems, too, that sporting participation when young affects sporting participation when older, so family, school and media influences can be long-lasting. Scheerder et al. (2006) found that active participation in sport by adolescents affected their level of sporting participation as adults. The study involved female participants and was a longitudinal one that used interviewing. The researchers found a correlation between sporting participation when younger and sporting participation as adults.

Tip
Scheerder et al. (2006) is an example of the use of correlation, so you can use it when discussing methodology.

Youth sport programmes seem to prepare the individual for adult participation in sport and this suggests that socialisation when young affects adult behaviour. Not only does socialisation affect sporting participation but also sporting participation can affect social-isation. For example, team playing can affect how children interact with one another and they can learn about leaders, followers, fair play, turn-taking and cooperation.

Socialisation and sporting performance
Parental influence seems to affect sporting success. Children repeat behaviour that is reinforced, for example, so parental encouragement is likely to lead to more practice and participation, which is likely to affect performance as well. Hellstedt (1998) suggests that medium parental involvement leads to the best likelihood of sporting success. Involvement includes paying the cost of training and transportation, as well as providing a role model to be imitated.

Evaluation of the effect of socialisation on sporting participation and performance
Strengths
- Evidence suggests that cultural norms are followed with regard to sport, such as 'male' or 'female' participation in certain sports, or 'gendering' of sports as found by Koivula (1995). This is evidence that socialisation processes affect sporting participation.
- Questionnaires are repeated and obtain similar results, so the findings are thought to be reliable. An example is the BSRI used by Koivula (1995).

Weaknesses
- Socialisation is a broad concept about the importance of nurture. It is hard to prove its influence, as 'nature' factors (such as personality) are also likely to affect both participation and performance. It is also hard to separate nurture and nature.

- Correlational analysis helps to show relationships between variables, as in Scheerder et al. (2006), for instance. However, it is hard to show cause-and-effect links. For example, adolescent behaviour may seem to predict adult behaviour with regard to sport. However, nature factors in adolescents are likely to affect them when adults as well.

Two theories of motivation

You need to cover achievement motivation as a theory as well as one other. Here the other theory covered is self-efficacy.

> **Tip**
>
> If you chose a different second theory of motivation, then you might prefer to revise that one rather than learn another one.

Defining motivation

Motivation refers to the reasons why someone behaves in a certain way and is thought of as either intrinsic or extrinsic. With **intrinsic motivation** (a key term), the drive to behave in a certain way comes from within a person; for example, from personality or inner drive. In sport, enjoying taking part would be intrinsic motivation. With **extrinsic motivation** (a key term), the reason for behaving in a certain way comes from outside the person; for example, from a financial reward or the praise of someone else. In sport, being cheered on would be extrinsic motivation. **Positive motivation** includes the need for achievement, the need for affiliation and the need for power. **Negative motivation** includes the need to avoid failure.

The achievement motivation theory: the McClelland–Atkinson model

In achievement motivation, the reason for doing something comes from a need to achieve success. The McClelland–Atkinson theory of motivation suggests that achievement motivation involves motivation to succeed and also fear of failure.

The model refers to the need for achievement (N-Ach), which involves having high standards and a high desire to master skills and to do well. Those with a high need for achievement choose reasonably difficult tasks that are challenging but also possible to achieve. They do not choose easy tasks or very difficult ones. High need for achievement seems to come from internal strength, praise for success and parents who encouraged independence.

McClelland carried out studies looking at the need for achievement. One study asked people to throw a hoop over a peg. Those with a high need for achievement stood at a distance which made the task not too hard and not too easy. This would help them to achieve mastery over the task. Those with a low need for achievement stood randomly at different distances.

The McClelland–Atkinson model suggests that:

achievement motivation = intrinsic motivation/fear of failure

Later work on the model added extrinsic motivation as a feature of achievement motivation and also fear of success.

Studies found that women seemed less motivated to succeed in sport than men, and it was this that led to the addition of fear of success to the model. However, it was suggested that women are less motivated because of social norms and the masculinity of sport, rather than because they fear success. The Bem Sex Role Inventory (BSRI) has been used to study gender differences in achievement motivation, and it was found that those who were more androgynous had higher achievement motivation (see p. 45 for an explanation of the BSRI and androgyny). This suggested that characters who were further away from being 'feminine' had higher achievement motivation.

Evaluation of achievement motivation theories
Strengths
- Achievement motivation theory fits well with the theory that socialisation affects sporting performance and participation, as it refers to how achievement motivation differs between genders, and learning could be involved. For example, females are less featured in sport in the media so women might not learn a desire to succeed from role models.
- Findings about achievement motivation have come from studies done in the West, where culture tends to be individualist and individual achievement is valued. In places where the culture is more collectivist, such as China, social achievement is valued more (e.g. Bond 1986). This suggests that cultural norms affect motivation, which supports the idea that achievement motivation is not biologically determined but relates as well to extrinsic motivation, fear of success and fear of failure.
- People in China, given the different focus on motivation, might be expected to succeed more in team sports rather than individual ones, and this has been found to be the case. This is evidence for the idea that the need to achieve is linked to socialisation and cultural norms.

Weaknesses
- Self-report data are used in questionnaires to rate sense of achievement or fear of success or failure. Self-report data can be unreliable, as responses can be affected by mood and other factors, such as when the survey is administered.
- Self-report data involve attitudes and opinions of the individual, which may not be a valid way to measure actual behaviour, such as sporting performance or participation in sport.
- The model may not predict behaviour and so has limited application.

Self-efficacy theory
A different theory which is used to explain motivation in sport is self-efficacy theory. Self-efficacy links to self-confidence, and self-confidence links with achievement motivation, but self-efficacy is a different theory.

Self-efficacy refers to the belief someone has that they can achieve well in a task and are competent. Efficacy is the power to bring about an effect; self-efficacy is about how far an individual feels they have that power, even if they do not. If someone has high self-efficacy for a task they will take it on, and if not they might avoid the task.

Self-efficacy includes self-confidence but is different — someone might have high self-efficacy with regard to one task and low self-efficacy with regard to another, so it is not a personality trait as such. Self-efficacy is also different from self-esteem: self-esteem concerns how someone feels about their self-worth in general, whereas self-efficacy refers to what they feel about their competence in a particular situation. If someone has low self-efficacy in a task, this may not affect their self-esteem because they might not invest their self-esteem in that task. For example, they may think they are no good at playing snooker but their self-esteem might not rest on them playing good snooker.

Bandura's social cognitive theory and self-efficacy

Bandura's social cognitive theory looks at the link between behaviour, the environment and cognitive factors. Bandura suggested that those with high self-efficacy tend to think they have control, whereas those with low self-efficacy do not. Factors affecting self-efficacy include:

- past performance accomplishments
- vicarious experiences — watching someone else do well and thinking that means they too can do well
- social persuasion — encouragement from others
- physiology and emotional state — interpreting feelings of arousal and so on

An important factor is performance. One bad performance might not affect self-efficacy, but in general, if someone does badly at something, they will have low self-efficacy because they will think they are not going to do well again.

The optimum level of self-efficacy is just above the level of ability because it will encourage people to try to do better and to achieve just above their ability. Low self-efficacy can be helpful if it encourages planning and persistence.

Conner and Norman (2005) suggested that behaviours such as not smoking depend on perceived self-efficacy, as do sporting behaviours.

Evaluation of self-efficacy theory

Strengths	Weaknesses
The theory has useful applications for helping performance.	The theory was tested on social learning and not on the learning of motor skills.
Experiments have used the ideas in an educational environment for the learning of skills and have shown that the ideas work; the theory has predictive power.	Self-report date can lack both reliability and validity.

Two theories looking at the effects of arousal, anxiety and the audience

This section explains the inverted U hypothesis about arousal and anxiety, and also evaluation apprehension theory, as the second theory needed in the course.

> **Tip**
>
> If you have learned about a different 'second' theory of arousal, anxiety and the audience effect, then you might prefer to revise that here instead of learning a new one. Make sure your two theories (inverted U and one other) cover all three areas — arousal, anxiety and the audience effect. Your course requires all three to be covered.

The inverted U hypothesis

The inverted U hypothesis is a theory about arousal and anxiety, and is used in sport psychology, as well as in other areas such as clinical psychology.

Arousal and the inverted U

Arousal is both a physiological (physical) and psychological state that involves areas of the brain and the autonomic nervous system. Arousal basically involves the fight or flight response (sometimes called 'flight, fight and freeze'), which is the body's response to threat, when the person goes 'on alert' and the body gets ready for action. The features of arousal include raised blood sugar, dry mouth, raised blood pressure, increased heart rate and other changes.

The **Yerkes–Dodson law** (1908) states that performance and arousal work together to give an inverted U shape — hence 'the inverted U hypothesis'. As arousal rises, performance rises, until at a certain level of arousal the situation reverses — as arousal rises even further, performance drops. Sports that require skill and precision (such as golf) need low arousal for optimum performance, whereas sports that require less precision and more strength (such as wrestling) need higher arousal for optimum performance. Simple tasks seem to be done better with high arousal, while more complex tasks are performed better with low arousal.

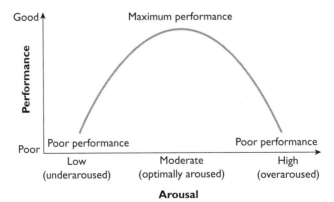

The inverted U hypothesis suggests that performance rises as arousal rises up to a certain point, after which continued arousal will cause performance to deteriorate

Anxiety and the inverted U

Anxiety is related to arousal — the physiological aspect of anxiety is arousal. However, with regard to its psychological element, anxiety is more related to emotions than arousal. Emotions such as fear and negative thoughts (e.g. about not being able to cope) produce anxiety, with the physiological response of arousal as well. Anxiety comes from areas of the brain rather than from the autonomic nervous system; for example, fear emotion from the amygdala.

Anxiety in sport is about the biological, cognitive, behavioural and emotional aspects of performance. Anxiety includes arousal and adds more. 'Worry' is the cognitive element of anxiety, including whether someone thinks they have the resources to cope with a situation. If someone does not think they have these resources, they experience stress.

Somatic anxiety refers to the physical features (arousal) and cognitive anxiety refers to anxious thoughts. The inverted U explains somatic anxiety in suggesting that a certain amount of somatic anxiety is good for performance but too much somatic anxiety means performance deteriorates. Cognitive anxiety always affects performance negatively, with no initial benefit. The theory which divides anxiety into somatic and cognitive anxiety is called the multi-dimensional theory.

Evaluation of the inverted U hypothesis

Strengths	Weaknesses
The inverted U goes further than drive theory and explains real-life observational data.	The main hypothesis needs extending to take account of the type of task and the experience of the performer.
The multi-dimensional anxiety theory also uses the idea of an inverted U, which gives support to the hypothesis.	It is difficult to separate anxiety and arousal; theories talk about them separately, so it is hard to link findings from both to form an explanation.

Evaluation apprehension theory

A second theory of arousal, anxiety and the audience effect is evaluation apprehension theory. The inverted U hypothesis concerns arousal and anxiety, while evaluation apprehension theory is about the effect of the audience on performance.

The **audience effect** refers to the effect of people being present (mere presence of others) and the effect of people watching and perhaps judging the performance. When having others present improves performance, this is social facilitation; there is also the co-actor effect, which refers to the effect on performance of other competitors.

Cottrell's evaluation apprehension theory

Cottrell (1968) looked at the audience effect on performance, focusing on the type of audience rather than the type of task. He focused specifically on whether others were just there (mere presence) or were watching and evaluating the performance. He found that performers were apprehensive about being watched and this apprehension was about being evaluated by others — hence the 'evaluation apprehension theory'.

The theory links to arousal in that apprehension raises levels of arousal and anxiety. There are links as well to the level of the performer (and perhaps self-efficacy). A beginner may be more apprehensive about being judged, so may experience more arousal than a more experienced performer.

> **Tip**
>
> Cottrell's (1968) study is one that you can choose to study in detail for your course, which would help in understanding evaluation apprehension theory, though that study is not explained in detail in this book.

Evidence for the audience effect

Michaels et al. (1982) found that pool players of above average ability achieved 69% of their shots when playing alone but 80% when a group of four people watched them. Below average pool players achieved about 36% of their shots alone and only 25% when watched by four people.

When someone is good at the task, the correct response is the **dominant response**, and when someone is not good, the wrong response is the dominant response. The Michaels et al. (1982) study shows that having an audience affects performance and affects it differently depending on ability. The dominant response is what occurs when there is arousal, and an audience seems to produce arousal. However, the Michaels et al. study did not look at whether the audience was evaluating performance or just there (mere presence of others).

Evidence for evaluation apprehension: Bartis et al. (1988)

Bartis et al. (1988) tested the evaluation apprehension theory. The study looked at whether the presence of an audience improved performance on a simple task but made performance on a complex task worse.

Some participants were asked to think of uses for a knife (the simple task) and others were asked to think of creative uses for a knife (the complex task). In the simple task, the correct response would be dominant and in the complex task, an incorrect response would be dominant. One half of each group was told that they would be individually identified and one was told their results would be anonymous. This was to test conditions where there was evaluation apprehension (their results being identified) or not (being anonymous).

The findings were as follows. In the simple task, those who thought they were being evaluated thought up more uses for the knife than in the group that were not made apprehensive (they would be anonymous). In the complex task, those who thought they would be anonymous thought of more creative uses for a knife than those in the evaluation apprehension condition.

It was concluded that evaluation apprehension helps with a simple task but hinders with a complex task. However, the study was not related to sport and also lacked validity, as it was not a naturalistic study.

Evaluation of evaluation apprehension theory: links to the inverted U

- When the dominant response is incorrect (a hard task) then there is likely to be more arousal than if the dominant response is correct (an easy task).
- Fear of being evaluated by an audience will increase arousal (and anxiety).
- So with an audience, someone not good at a task will experience a lot of arousal and, in accordance with the inverted U hypothesis, as arousal increases perform-ance will fall.
- These findings can be explained by the evaluation apprehension theory — in a simple task, performance is enhanced by fear of being evaluated (some arousal is good), but in a complex task, performance is made worse by fear of being evalu-ated (too much arousal is not good).
- However, the findings can also be explained by the inverted U hypothesis.

Strengths and weaknesses of the evaluation apprehension theory

Strengths	Weaknesses
Findings match the inverted U hypothesis findings about arousal.	Laboratory studies like Bartis et al. (1988) lack ecological validity.
Experiments give reliable findings.	Laboratory studies lack validity with regard to the task.
	It is hard to operationalise fear of being evaluated in order to test it.

Two psychological techniques for improving performance in sport

This section discusses imagery and goal-setting as two techniques for improving performance in sport.

Tips

- If you have studied different techniques for improving sporting performance, you may prefer to revise them rather than learn the ones explained here.
- Imagery relates to the Boyd and Munroe (2003) study that you have to cover for this course.

Using imagery to improve performance

Imagery refers to the creation of mental perceptions of aspects of an experience that would be there in the real experience. Imagery often involves visualisation but can also include auditory or kinaesthetic (body position and touch) features. For example, a sportsperson can imagine the roar of the crowd or see themselves jumping the required height.

The idea is to create a mental representation of what is required and what the athlete wants to achieve, such as winning a race or achieving a personal best. An athlete might also want to visualise resting as well as competing. The aim is for the athlete to imagine a scenario and then 'step into' that feeling.

Imagery is used to practise skills, to improve confidence, and to control anxiety and arousal. Boyd and Munroe (2003) (pp. 42–44) looked at how climbers used imagery, for example to work out a plan for a climb, and how track and field athletes used imagery to visualise winning. Studies often use the five functions of imagery as a framework (p. 42).

Studies of use of imagery in sport

Feltz and Landers (1983) carried out a meta-analysis of 60 studies where half the participants used mental practice and the other half acted as a control (no mental practice). They found in general that mental practice was better than no practice but not as good as physical (actual) practice.

Martin and Hall (1995) looked at the use of imagery in golf. Thirty-nine beginners were split into two groups, with one group using imagery and the other acting as a control group. They were all taught how to hit golf balls. The imagery group were found to be more realistic in their expectations, to stick to their training more, and to set higher goals for themselves. It was concluded that using imagery affects motivation as well as performance.

It is generally thought that visual imagery is more effective than no physical practice but is not as good as physical practice. A mixture of mental and physical practice can improve performance and visual imagery can improve motivation.

Evaluation of the use of imagery to improve performance

Strengths
- Mental practice seems to work, and studies such as Feltz and Landers (1983) seem to give evidence for this.
- Studies tend to be experiments with the use of a control group, so are replicable. Findings tend to support one another, which gives reliability, and the controls allow cause-and-effect conclusions to be drawn.

Weaknesses
- Studies tend to be experiments and often involve novices in a sport as well, so the findings might lack validity.
- Such studies do not include the pressure of the sporting situation or the influence of an audience, which have been shown to affect peformance.

Using goal-setting to improve performance

Goal-setting involves focusing on what is desired and working out how to achieve that goal. This is a mental process and to an extent involves imagery. Goal-setting theory has three main principles:
- Setting difficult goals leads to higher performance than setting easy ones.
- Specific goals lead to higher performance than general goals.
- Feedback on performance is very important.

Goals must be clear and attainable and there must be a way of measuring them. The individual must accept the goal and be involved in setting the goal so that they are committed. Rewarding achievement is important, and extrinsic rewards are often useful in addition to intrinsic ones.

Goals should be specific, measurable, adjustable, realistic and time-limited (SMART). Goals that lead to self-improvement are thought to be more successful than goals such as 'beating an opponent'.

A study on goal setting and performance: Mellalieu et al. (2006)

Mellalieu et al. (2006) looked at five male rugby players at national collegiate level aged between 21 and 24, studying their performance over a season. The study was done in Wales. The players had set their own goals and targets, and the study was to see if goals set by players led to better performance.

Rugby behaviours were measured, such as successful kicks, number of successful turnovers won, number of tackles made or number of times a player moved forward with the ball in his hand. Matches were filmed and such behaviours added up.

The study covered 20 games over one season and the first ten were studied to give a baseline measure. The behaviour each player wanted to change was chosen by them at the start of the season, so that the baseline measures obtained from the first ten games focused on that behaviour for each player (they chose different aspects of the game). Then, in the break before the next ten matches, interventions were put in place, with the players setting their goals for the second half of the season (e.g. a specific number of tackles to be attempted). The goals were also reviewed before each of the next ten matches.

Results showed that in those last ten games of the season (the second half) participant 1 improved in ball carries by 77%, participant 2 made 32% more tackles, participant 3 decreased the number of missed tackles by 55%, participant 4 improved successful kicks by 26% and participant 5 improved turnovers won by 118%.

Evaluation of Mellalieu et al. (2006)

Strengths
- The study took place in the field (in natural surroundings), so there was validity.
- The baseline measure was carefully carried out so that the percentage improvement could be clearly measured using quantitative data.

Weaknesses
- The measurements were precise, but other factors, such as the weather and the strength of the opposition, would also be likely to affect behaviour.
- Taking part in the study may have led to changes in the players' behaviour, although it could be suggested that the behaviour in the first ten games might also be affected by being part of the study.
- Only five participants and one sport were involved, so generalising might not be appropriate.

Evaluation of the use of goal-setting to improve performance
Strengths
- Goal-setting uses measurable goals and studies tend to be replicable.
- The individual is involved in goal-setting and goals are not imposed, so the technique is ethical and fair.

Weaknesses
- A lot of the research has been done using college students, which might limit generalisation.
- Research tends to be laboratory-based so findings tend to lack validity (though Mellalieu et al. 2006 use a field setting).
- Goal-setting includes imagery and focus on motivation, making it hard to separate goal-setting from other techniques.

Studies in detail

Boyd and Munroe (2003) is the study in detail set for this application, and then there is a choice of one from three others. In this book, the other study in detail is Koivula (1995), but mention has also been made of Craft et al. (2003) (pp. 49–50) and Cottrell (1968) (pp. 62–63).

Boyd and Munroe (2003) (pp. 42–44) and Koivula (1995) (pp. 44–46) were explained in detail in the methodology section.

Evidence in practice: key issue and practical

In this section the key issue considered is gender differences in sport and in particular, how there is more focus on male sport than on female sport.

> **Tip**
>
> If you studied a different key issue, you might prefer to revise that instead of learning about a new one. You need to use your own practical as you will be asked, for example, about how you found the information, how you carried out the analysis, what problems you came across and what results you found.

Gender differences in sport

Koivula (1995) (pp. 44–46) showed that people 'gender' sport and that, although many sports are seen as 'neutral', quite a high number are seen as 'male' and fewer as 'female'. She suggested that socialisation and gender-based schematic information processing mean that sport is seen in terms of appropriateness for the different genders and that people perceive gender in a certain way as well. Socialisation is an explanation for sporting participation and sporting performance (pp. 56–58).

The issue is why male sport is more often mentioned in the media than female sport. For example, female cricket and female rugby are rarely shown or mentioned on television but the male versions are covered extensively. In schools both girls and boys do sport, so it is surprising perhaps that adult sport focuses so much on males.

Practical

You will need to use the practical you carried out. With regard to male and female sport in the media, one idea for a content analysis is to use the sporting pages of a newspaper (or more than one on different days perhaps) and count the number of times sportsmen (or male sport) and sportswomen (or female sport) are mentioned. Then an analysis of the data can be carried out to see if there is a difference.

Questions
&
Answers

This part of the guide presents questions for each of the two applications, first for Health Psychology and then for Sport Psychology. For each application, the questions are divided into five sections, one for each area of the specification:

- Definition of the application
- Methodology and how science works
- Content
- Studies in detail
- Evidence in practice: key issue and practical

Choose one area of the specification and revise the material using this unit guide. Work through the questions for your chosen area, answering them yourself without reading the advice on how to answer the question and without reading the answers given. Then mark your own answers, and read through the advice on what is required. Did you interpret the question successfully? Read through the answers given and note where the marks are awarded. Finally, read through the examiner's comments to see what a full answer should include.

Examiner's comments

All questions and answers are followed by examiner's comments. These are preceded by the icon e. The comments on the questions suggest what is required in an answer and point out important features of the question, such as where there is more than one issue to focus on. The comments on the answer indicate where credit is due and point out areas for improvement, specific problems and common errors, such as poor time management, lack of clarity, weak or non-existent development, irrelevance, misinterpretation of the question and mistaken meanings of terms.

Health psychology
Definition of the application

(a) **Explain what is meant by both physical and psychological dependence.** (4 marks)

(b) **Jane is a health psychologist and is asked what her job entails. She only has a few minutes to answer, so decides to outline one area of her work. Outline one area that Jane might cover in her work.** (4 marks)

> (a) This question could give 2 marks each for definitions of the terms — however, it asks you to explain both types of dependence so it is more likely that the overall answer will get the 4 marks. Make sure you say what both mean, and then one way of getting the full marks would be to give an example of both, using one drug perhaps.
>
> (b) When stimulus material like this is given, make sure you refer to the material at least once, which can be done here just by mentioning Jane. The question asks you to outline one area that a health psychologist might cover. As you have covered substance misuse in your course, that is a good area to cover in your answer, although health psychology also covers many other areas.

■ ■ ■

Answers

(a) Physical dependence when referring to substance misuse means when typical functioning for the individual is not possible without them taking the substance. ✓ They are dependent on the substance for normal functioning and this is addiction. Physical dependence also means that if someone stops taking the drug they will get withdrawal symptoms. ✓ Psychological dependence refers to when they cannot do without the drug, either for social support or to maintain a reasonable mental state. ✓ So, for example, someone might continue to take heroin to stop them shaking or to prevent other withdrawal symptoms, which shows they are physically dependent on heroin. ✓ They might continue to take the drug to give them a mental state where they can cope with everyday living, and this shows psychological dependence.

> There are 4 marks here, as indicated by the ticks. You can see that the answer gets just 1 mark for the information on psychological dependence and 3 for physical dependence, which is fine as overall it gets the full marks.

(b) As a health psychologist Jane might be involved in putting together a campaign against misuse of a certain drug, or drugs in general. Health psychology gives information about what an addict will need to do to stop taking the drug and a campaign can be targeted specifically. ✓ For example, methadone treatment can help heroin addicts so places where such treatment is available can be advertised in areas where heroin addicts are found. ✓ However, health psychologists suggest

question

that drug treatment alone might not be enough, as it targets physical dependence only, and psychological dependence also needs to be addressed. ✓ So counselling can be offered in the treatment centres and advertised alongside the drug treatment. ✓ Peer pressure can also affect drug taking, so a campaign can involve addicts who have stopped taking heroin and who can explain how it felt to give up, how hard it was, or what strategies they used. ✓

The detail here is sufficient — in fact, there are 5 marks for a 4-mark question. The answer brings in areas of understanding that include explanations for drug taking, such as biological and social explanations. There is also mention of how drug treatment alone is probably not enough. When using questions to practise before the exam, it is good to give more than you need — in an exam you are likely to forget things, so if you know more than you need, you can then still get full marks.

Methodology and how science works

(a) Outline how animals are used in experiments to study substance misuse. (4 marks)

(b) Explain how two different research methods have been used with humans in the study of substance misuse. (6 marks)

(a) This question asks about the use of animals in experiments, but there is a focus on how substance misuse is studied using animals. It would be best to comment on that particular area at least once, if not more.

(b) Assume that there are 3 marks for each research method and make sure that the methods involve using humans as participants and not animals. Bring in some examples of the use of the methods in looking at substance misuse. General points about the methods can also gain credit.

■ ■ ■

Answers

(a) Experiments using animals are well controlled and take place in an artificial setting where the environment of the animals is carefully monitored. ✓ One aspect of the study will be manipulated, which is the independent variable, and another variable will be measured as a result of that manipulation; this will be the dependent variable. ✓ For example, if monkeys are offered a recreational drug or water, studies show that they choose the drug, which suggests that the drug is reinforcing. ✓

This answer has been given 3 marks, not the full 4 marks. Some more detail about the studies using monkeys would be useful, or perhaps another example of how animals are used in experiments to study substance misuse. Pickens and Thompson (1968) was a study in the AS course that you may have covered when looking at the learning approach. The study looked at rats and the effects of cocaine and could be included here. Focus on animals, not just experiments.

(b) Questionnaires are used in the study of substance misuse, for example to find out about smoking habits in young people. Ennett et al. (1994) used questionnaires to find out about smoking habits and also to find out about friendship patterns, to see if peer groups affected smoking behaviour. ✓ The questionnaires were self-administered and 1,092 students completed them. Five different schools were surveyed and friends within the schools were put into groups according to who said they were friends with whom. ✓ Questionnaires tend to focus on quantitative data so that numbers can be compared and so that data are easily analysed, such as a list of friends. ✓

Interviews are also used to find out about drug use. Interviews were used in Blättler et al. (2002), at the start of the study and again every 6 months up to the eighteenth month. ✓ This was a longitudinal study. Questions were asked about the use of both heroin and cocaine as well as about lifestyle. ✓ The questions were backed

question

up by physiological measures as well, to check whether the answers were truthful (such as whether the person was still taking heroin and/or cocaine). ✓

This answer has focused on two methods by using two different studies, which is fine. There is not much about the methods in general but more about how they were used specifically in the two studies, which is one way of answering the question. There is quite a bit of detail. The final mark is for showing that interviewing might need to be supplemented with data from other sources as well. This would not be a well-focused point with regard to a question about interviewing. However, for this question a specific issue about the use of interviewing in health psychology is relevant, and the example study is elaborated in the answer, so credit is given.

Content

(a) Describe and evaluate two explanations of substance misuse. (12 marks)

(b) Compare biological and learning explanations of substance misuse. (4 marks)

(c) Compare two ways of treating substance abuse. (6 marks)

(d) Outline one campaign that has encouraged people to stop using drugs. (3 marks)

(a) This is an essay question, which you can tell by the number of marks (essay questions are likely to have 12 marks). This means that the answer is marked using levels rather than point by point. Your answer is put into a band of marks — the top level, for example, is between 10 and 12 marks. At this level, the answer would have to be clearly communicated and use relevant terms appropriately. You would need to address all parts of the question (in this case both 'describe' and 'evaluate' two explanations) and to use evidence as appropriate.

When practising essays, however, it is useful to think of marking points just as in other questions, so that you can work on including enough material. So for this answer, ticks are in brackets to indicate suitable marking points. You need to describe two explanations of drug abuse, for around 3 or 4 marks each, and then to evaluate both, again for about 4 marks each. To evaluate, you could compare the two explanations or you could use evidence from studies. Giving evidence from studies involves evaluation because it is supporting the theory (or failing to do so) — suggesting that 'this theory is right (or wrong) because there is this evidence…', which is an evaluative point.

Although it is suggested here that you try to get around 4 marks each for the two descriptions and the two evaluations (which would be 16 marks), remember that in practice the marking will use the levels. An example of the levels can be found in the specimen assessment materials (SAMs), which are on the e-spec that goes with the course and also on the Edexcel website.

(b) When comparing, look at similarities and differences; for 4 marks give four comparison points. Be sure to make each point fully: for example, don't suggest a difference and add 'the other one does not' — say fully how the two are different. For similarities and differences you could consider the methodology. For example, you could consider if the same research methods are used (a similarity) or different ones (a difference), or whether animals are used in both (a similarity) or one explanation tends to get evidence from animals and the other from humans (a difference).

(c) Having 6 marks for this sort of question makes it quite difficult and comparison questions can be hard if not prepared. To find similarities and differences, think of strengths and weaknesses of the two treatments. Consider the approach they are from or the research methods used to find evidence for them or from which they are derived. Ethical issues can be useful as well, as perhaps one treatment is seen as more ethical than another one.

(d) You need to focus on a particular campaign rather than a general campaign (e.g. not the general campaign to stop smoking, but a particular one). The actual campaign itself needs to be outlined here.

■ ■ ■

Answers

(a) One major explanation for substance misuse is a biological one, which explains how drugs work at the synapse in the brain. Drugs are chemicals and they work in the brain to give a pleasurable reaction and for some drugs an addiction reaction as well. (✓ — description) Messages are sent in the brain using synaptic transmission, which is when an electrical impulse travels down the axon of a neuron and reaches terminal buttons at the end of the axon. (✓— description) The impulse triggers the release of a neurotransmitter, which enters the synaptic gap at the end of the neuron (the terminal buttons are at the end). (✓ — description) That neurotransmitter is picked up by receptors at the dendrites of an adjacent neuron (if the chemical fits the receptors). This then triggers a signal in that adjacent neuron. Drugs act like neurotransmitters at the synapse and either send messages or block the receptors so that messages are not sent. (✓ — description)

Evidence from studies with mice shows that heroin works like morphine and acts on opioid receptors and changes are brought about in receptors, so this is evidence that heroin affects the brain at the synapse. (✓ — evaluation) Both dopamine and serotonin are involved in drug misuse and addiction and these are the neurotransmitters linked to pleasure and positive emotions, which again is evidence for the biological explanation. (✓ — evaluation) Blum et al. (1996) suggested that problems with the dopamine system might be what leads some people to seek more pleasure, which might explain why some people are more likely to become addicted than others. (✓ — evaluation)

Another explanation for substance misuse is that addiction comes from social learning, with role models being imitated. Social learning theory suggests that behaviour is imitated if a role model is similar to the individual, (✓ — description) if the behaviour is attended to and observed, if the behaviour is remembered and if there is motivation to repeat the behaviour. So there might be peer group pressure that, for example, leads someone to drink alcohol or smoke cigarettes — or to use other recreational drugs. (✓ — description) Those who are imitated tend to be those who are important to the individual, such as significant others like parents or friends, or someone the person identifies with such as a media celebrity or sportsperson. (✓ — description) The actual drug that is used can depend on the group; younger adolescents seem to be more susceptible than older ones and it can depend on how much exposure the individual has to the 'drug scene'. (✓ — description)

Bandura's studies into social learning have shown that adult behaviour is watched and repeated; however, many studies are laboratory experiments so there might not be validity in the findings. For example, studies have children watching adult behaviour and then playing and being observed to see if that behaviour is repeated. This does not account for long-term learning of behaviour, only short-term learning. (✓ — evaluation) Social learning has been shown in animals: for example, monkeys that are trained to be afraid of washing-up liquid bottles can model this behaviour and cause other monkeys to be afraid in the same way. (✓ — evaluation) Ennett et al. (1994) showed that young people did not have 'smoking' peer groups or friendship cliques but that in fact most cliques were non-smoking, so it did not seem as if smoking is linked to peer pressure. (✓ — evaluation)

> Although there are not quite 4 marking points for each of the four areas (describing the two explanations and evaluating them), there is enough here for full marks to be likely. Evidence is used well as evaluation, including giving named studies, which shows a good level. Terms are well used throughout.

(b) The biological explanation that says that synaptic transmission is what causes tolerance and addiction gets evidence from animal studies, and social learning theory gets evidence from humans and animals, but mainly humans. ✓ This is because social learning involves cognitive processes such as remembering, identifying and being motivated, and humans need to be involved to test such issues. (✓ — elaboration) Social learning theory rests on nurture explanations, because it focuses on the influence of the environment, whereas biological explanations look at nature, because they are about the organism and how it functions rather than environmental influences. ✓ Both social learning theory and biological explanations use laboratory experiments to gather data, so both rest on scientific evidence from controlled studies. ✓ Drug treatment programmes tend to work with regard to helping someone give up taking the drug (such as heroin); however, they are shown to work better if the environment is also dealt with (such as the presence of a peer group), so it seems as if both explanations are needed. It may not be that they should be compared as if one or the other is right, but that both are useful. ✓

> There are 5 marks here at least (because the mark is often given after the point has been clearly elaborated whereas it could be given sooner), so this answer would be expected to get the full 4 marks. The answer is thorough, and a range of similarities and differences are given, as well as the useful point at the end that suggests that comparing the two is perhaps not appropriate, as both might have something to offer. This is not quite a comparison point but is relevant to the answer so is given credit. However, it might be advisable to stick to pure comparisons and give one sentence per comparison point to make sure you are focusing precisely on the question.

(c) Drug treatment for substance misuse uses a medical model, in that treatment is done at a clinic and by using substances to treat the substance misuse. Token economy can also be within a medical model, as it is used in institutions like hospitals to encourage suitable behaviour in an addict. ✓ However, token economy can also be used outside an institution whereas drug treatment would need to be prescribed and monitored. ✓ Token economy comes from learning principles and operant conditioning, whereas drug treatment comes from the biological approach and information about how the brain works. ✓ So token economy is about nurture and using principles about the effects of the environment to overcome drug addiction, whereas drug treatment is about nature and uses principles of how the brain works to overcome addiction. ✓ Both token economy and drug treatment come from principles found by using animals in laboratory experiments in controlled conditions, so both would be seen as scientific treatments. ✓ This contrasts with cognitive behavioural therapy, for example, or other types of psychotherapy, which tend to rely on the less scientific ideas of those such as Freud and Rogers, though there are behavioural principles involved in CBT. (✓ — elaboration)

   There are 6 marks here and 5 are clearly comparison points. The final mark is a contrasting explanation and elaborates on the idea that the two chosen treatments are 'scientific', so a mark is given for the elaboration of the previous point.

(d) The British Heart Foundation in 2008 instigated an anti-smoking campaign that included posters and a website. The campaign used posters that intended to shock and the focus was on how smoking causes heart damage and heart attacks. ✓ It is thought that the best thing someone can do to help to prevent a heart attack is to stop smoking and the BHF wanted to get that message out to all smokers. The campaign focused on fear, given by the posters, ✓ and support, given on the website. Information was there about how to find support groups and replacement therapy (such as patches). ✓

   There is enough here for the 3 marks as quite a bit is explained about the campaign itself. The ticks show that you need to explain in quite good detail before a mark is given.

Studies in detail

(a) What did Blättler et al. (2002) conclude from their study? (3 marks)

(b) In your study of health psychology, you will have covered one other study focusing on substance abuse other than heroin abuse. Describe and evaluate this other study. (12 marks)

(a) This is the same as asking for the conclusions of the study for 3 marks but you can also give something about the results in order to clarify the conclusions. This would help if you don't know enough detail with regard to conclusions alone.

(b) You may have looked at many studies other than Blättler et al. (2002) but this question is focusing on your other 'study in detail' so it is best to use that. You could use any other study as long as you know enough about it. In this book the other study in detail is Ennett et al. (1994) pp. 36–37, which looks at smoking behaviour, so that study is used here. This is an essay question, so refer to the comments on question 3(a) in Section 3 of Health Psychology (p. 75) for more information about how to answer an essay question and how an essay answer is marked. Ticks are given here in brackets but the marking uses levels, so you do not have to give a certain number of points — it is the quality of your answer that gets credit as well as the quantity.

■ ■ ■

Answers

(a) There were 16% of the sample who did not use cocaine at the start of the study and by the end of the study, 52% did not use cocaine, so it was reasonable to conclude that the treatment for heroin was successful in stopping the use of cocaine, which was what the study set out to find. ✓ The number of daily users of cocaine fell from 30% at the baseline measure to 6% at the end, which is a large fall and also suggests that drug treatment for heroin will also help the same people give up cocaine, so will help with regard to poly-drug use. ✓ 75% of the urine tests were negative for cocaine so this also shows that cocaine use was affected by the treatment. It was also concluded that those who continued to use cocaine (i.e. those for whom the treatment did not work) were those whose behaviour linked to prostitution, illicit heroin use, illegal income and contact with the drug scene — so where the treatment did not seem to work, there were other factors that might have led to this lack of success. ✓

The answer uses results, which are not creditable in themselves, but then concludes from the results, which is creditable. There is a lot of useful detail and there are clearly 3 marks, if not more.

(b) Ennett et al. (1994) aimed to see if smoking behaviour goes with friendship cliques in adolescents in the USA. The aim was to gather information about friendships

question

and draw up friendship cliques. Then the researchers wanted to get information about smoking habits and see if the two related. (✓ — description) They used ninth-grade students (aged around 14 years) in one area of the USA in 1980 and, although data were gathered in that year, the researchers were careful to note that smoking habits had not changed in that time so they felt that the data were relevant in 1994. (✓ — description)

The young people filled in questionnaires that they were given and reported on their friendships and their smoking behaviour. Mothers also gave information about their level of education, which was one of the variables. (✓ — description) The study involved 1,092 participants and 87 friendship cliques in five schools in the area. A clique was made up of three or more adolescents who were connected by friendship paths. (✓ — description) A link between person A and person B was taken as a reciprocal link and given one point, and if person B had also said they were friends with person A then two points would be given, as this was a confirmed reciprocal link. (✓ — description)

Of the participants, 42.4% were clique members and the others were friends with other adolescents but not in the cliques, or isolates (not friends with clique members at all). (✓ — description) A Spearman's test was done to see if the more connected a clique was (the more links there were between members of a clique), the more similarity there would be with regard to smoking. (✓ — description) Of the cliques, 93% had between three and ten members, with average clique size being five. Very few cliques had both boys and girls in them or had both black and white members — cliques were found to be homogenous. (✓ — description) It was found that 89.8% of all clique members were non-smokers, 68% of cliques had only non-smokers as members and 2% of the cliques were made up entirely of smokers (two cliques). (✓ — description) It was concluded that adolescents who smoked tended to associate with one another, but most of the adolescents were non-smokers and few cliques were smoking cliques. So if peer groups accounted for smoking behaviour it was more to discourage smoking than to encourage it. (✓ — description)

The study was thought to be valid with regard to learning about cliques, as the data came directly from the friends themselves, although counting non-reciprocal links as reciprocal links may have affected the validity of the study. (✓ — evaluation) Adolescents had to list their three best friends too, which may have limited the data, and thus the validity of the data. (✓ — evaluation) Self-report data can be unreliable as well, because on a different occasion or in a different place, the replies to the questionnaire might have differed. (✓ — evaluation) Also, perhaps in particular with regard to issues such as smoking, the participants may not have wanted to admit to it or may have felt it was 'cool' to admit to it. (✓ — evaluation) In either case, this involves demand characteristics and might affect the validity of the data. This study was done in the USA, so findings might not generalise to other cultures where friendship patterns and/or smoking habits might be different. (✓ — evaluation)

There are a lot of description points and quite a few evaluation points here. The terms are appropriately used and there is a lot of detail about the study, including aims, procedure, results and conclusions. This would be a top-band essay (from 10 to 12 marks). Remember that, although ticks are given here in brackets to indicate marks, the actual marking would use levels.

Evidence in practice: key issue and practical

(a) Describe one key issue within health psychology that you have studied. (5 marks)

(b) The following questions concern the practical you carried out when studying health psychology. You will have carried out either a content analysis focusing on a key issue or a summary analysis of two sources focusing on a topic covered within the application. Answer the following questions with that analysis or summary in mind.

(i) How did you choose the topic for your summary analysis of two sources or for your content analysis? (2 marks)

(ii) What did you find out from your content analysis or summary analysis of two articles? (4 marks)

(a) There are 5 marks here for saying what the key issue is about without using psychology to explain it. You have to focus on material that you have covered in this application, so the key issue has to be about substance abuse in some way.

(b) (i) This question asks you to explain your focus in your practical and why you chose that focus. Answer specifically (do not just say that you chose it because it was your key issue). The marking is done using levels, not point by point. Questions on practicals are generally marked using levels because it is hard to predict what candidates will write about — the marking is more about quality than quantity or getting the 'right answer'.

(b) (ii) This question is asking for your findings, which can be results and/or conclusions. The question is quite general so could even be about methodological problems — for example, 'I found out that to do a content analysis I needed to find more than one source of information; otherwise I could only generalise to that one leaflet.'

■ ■ ■

Answers

(a) One key issue that concerns health psychologists is how to prevent drug abuse and another is how to treat it. For example, anti-smoking campaigns are often put into action. The British Heart Foundation in 2008 instigated an anti-smoking campaign that included posters and a website. The campaign used posters that intended to shock and the focus was on how smoking causes heart damage and heart attacks. ✓ It is thought that the best thing someone can do to help to prevent a heart attack is to stop smoking and the BHF wanted to get that message out to all smokers. The campaign focused on fear, given by the posters, ✓ and support, given on the website. Information was there about how to find support groups and replacement therapy (such as patches). ✓ Other such campaigns include posters to show the effects of prolonged use of heroin — Barnardos carried out such a campaign using a picture of a baby injecting itself (seemingly), which was an image calculated to shock parents and mothers into realising that drug-taking harms a growing foetus. ✓ One reason for having such campaigns is that drug-taking costs the health service and society money in treating drug addicts, so this is a key issue for society. Another reason is that society requires citizens that can contribute and can function fully, which it is thought those on drugs cannot do. ✓

📝 This answer gets the 5 marks and gives two good examples of ways to prevent drug abuse. The focus is on prevention rather than treatment so the focus matches the issue. After the useful examples, a few reasons are given as to why this is a key issue for society. It is important to include such an explanation in your answer.

(b) (i) I chose to find two articles about prevention of drug abuse because I wanted to find out why it was thought that prevention was necessary, given that in some cases — such as alcohol, smoking and cannabis — some people think that taking the drug is not such a bad thing.

📝 This is a useful answer because it gives a clear reason for looking at campaigns carried out to stop drug-taking and there is enough for the 2 marks.

(b) (ii) I found out that the two articles about stopping drug abuse were very similar, in that they both talked about the importance of peer groups in starting people taking drugs and in keeping up the addiction. Both suggested that education in schools in tutor groups would be useful because peer groups are often within one tutor group, so if there was open discussion about the issues of taking drugs, the tutor group members might help to support one another. However, one article thought that too much discussion about taking drugs might encourage it, as adolescents had the idea brought to their attention so might try it, whereas the other article promoted the idea of drug education in schools.

📝 This answer gives quite a bit of information but it is rather general and 3 marks seem more likely than the full 4 marks. Add more actual detail about the two articles, such as what the aims were concerning the prevention of drug-taking.

Sport psychology
Definition of the application

(a) **Complete the table below, explaining three areas that sport psychology covers by giving an explanation of what each term in the table means.** (3 marks)

Term	Explanation of the term as used in sport psychology
Excellence	This refers to how good a person is in their chosen sport and the idea that a sportsperson aims to be the best.
Performance	
Participation	
Motivation	

(b) **Adrian is a 13-year-old county-level swimmer who wants to get into the Olympic team for his country. The next Olympics are in 3 years' time. Adrian's mother feels that the county coach is not encouraging him enough. Adrian enjoys swimming but also likes going out with his friends. What is it about this issue that means that a sport psychologist might be involved?** (3 marks)

(a) The table would have more room for your answer in the exam. You need to write in what each of the three terms means with reference to sport psychology. The first answer is there to guide you. 'Performance' is not a key term but is used often in the course so you would be expected to know how the term is used in sport psychology. 'Motivation' is not a key term either but 'intrinsic motivation' and 'extrinsic motivation' are key terms, so again you would be expected to be able to define 'motivation' in terms of sport psychology. Note that these sorts of questions are perhaps not likely at A2, but it is as well to be aware that there are many different ways of asking questions, and you will be expected to be able to use your knowledge in a flexible way like this.

(b) This question is about what sport psychology is, and you need to explain the features of the source that make it relevant to sport psychology. There are 3 marks available, so try to make three clear points. Include Adrian, swimming, and/or Adrian's mother in your answer to show that you are focusing on the source.

■ ■ ■

Answers

(a)

Term	Explanation of the term as used in sport psychology
Excellence	This refers to how good a person is in their chosen sport and the idea that a sportsperson aims to be the best.
Performance	This refers to how good a person is in their sport, and is about how well they do in what circumstances, and what might improve how good they are at their sport.
Participation	This refers to which sports someone takes part in and this can depend, for example, on their gender because socialisation can affect which sports someone takes up and sport tends to be 'gendered' in a society.
Motivation	This refers to whether someone wants to take up a sport or to do well in that sport and how much drive they have to train and prepare. There is 'intrinsic motivation', which comes from within the individual (e.g. from pride), and there is 'extrinsic motivation', which comes from outside the individual (such as trophies and money).

> In all three cases there is easily enough for the 1 mark — enough really for 2 marks each. It is as well, though, to explain properly like this for all the points you make in the exam, as points have to be made clearly and effectively.

(b) Adrian wants to improve his swimming ability, which is about his performance, and he wants to achieve excellence, so as sport psychologists are involved in studying performance and how to improve it, this is how a sport psychologist might be involved. ✓ Adrian's mother is criticising the coaching and a sport psychologist is often involved in explaining what makes a good coach or in studying coaching techniques. ✓ Adrian likes going out with his friends perhaps, instead of swimming practice, and this is about motivation. Sport psychologists are involved in studying motivation, both intrinsic and extrinsic, to see how to improve motivation. ✓

> There are three clear ideas here, all picked up from the source, and this gives the 3 marks required. The source is used well and there is clear understanding of what sport psychology is, which is the focus of the question.

Methodology and how science works

(a) Explain ethical issues when using questionnaires as a research method in sport psychology. (3 marks)

(b) Asma wanted to find out about horseriders and how they dealt with nerves before a performance. She was particularly interested as she had recently attended a competition where she had wanted to ride but had not been able to, and she had witnessed a bad fall by one of the riders. She was going to use a questionnaire to ask riders about their fears and feelings before a performance and she was not sure whether she wanted to gather quantitative data, qualitative data or both.

Explain the advantages for Asma of using both sorts of data in the study. (4 marks)

(a) This question is asking for an evaluation of questionnaires in terms of ethics. As there is mention of sport psychology, any examples should focus on sport. There are 3 marks so you need to give three different points or elaborate to be sure of gaining full marks.

(b) Think about the study that Asma is planning and then write as if you were advising her about the value of the two types of data. Address both types and then comment on how it would be useful to use both types. Focus on Asma's needs, given the aims of her study.

■ ■ ■

Answers

(a) Questionnaires are a reasonably ethical research method because they are written questions where there is room to ensure that instructions are clear and confidentiality is clearly given. ✓ The participant can be told that no names are required, for example, and they can be informed almost completely about what the study is testing. ✓ It is possible that there might be some deception so that the focus of the study is not so obvious as to cause demand characteristics, and deception is unethical. However, this deception is slight as the overall aims of the study can usually be explained. ✓ For example, the climbers and track and field athletes in Boyd and Munroe's (2003) study could be informed that the questionnaire was about their performance in general, rather than about how good they were at the sport, and they could be told it was about how they prepared for their performance. ✓

This answer focuses on confidentiality, informed consent and deception, and explains how these link to questionnaires. There is good use of the example study as well, so there is enough for the 3 marks and perhaps a little more. It is a good idea to provide a little more, to be sure of getting full marks. Another issue could be the right to withdraw, which can be offered at the top of the questionnaire alongside instructions.

(b) Asma wants to know how the riders feel so she wants their opinions and their fears. This means she wants some rich and detailed information so that she can analyse the data and find themes that summarise how riders feel. This means she needs qualitative data, which give that sort of depth and detail. ✓ However, it would also be useful to generate some statements and find out how far the riders agree with them so that she has some figures to use. She could then use correlational analysis. ✓ For example, if she could find a 'fear' score and also a 'confidence' score (about how far the riders think they can succeed — perhaps this is about self-efficacy), then she could test whether the more confident a rider is, the less they feel fear. ✓ So quantitative data would also be useful. Qualitative data will add information about the type of fear or what makes someone confident, for example, whereas quantitative data can be analysed statistically to see if there is a relationship between fear and confidence, so Asma would do well to gather both sorts of data. ✓

> There are four ticks given here to show each place where there is enough information for a mark. The focus is clearly on Asma's study and also on the two types of data. It is clear that both types are understood and the examples (e.g. about fear and confidence) help to show understanding. The answer ends by showing why both types of data would be useful, which shows very good focus on the question.

uestion 8

Content

(a) **What effect do personality traits have on sporting participation?** (4 marks)

(b) **Outline one strength and one weakness of achievement motivation theory.** (4 marks)

(c) **Using the two terms given, label the two axes (for the scores going up and those going across) in the diagram of the inverted U theory.** (1 mark)

TERMS: Performance

Arousal

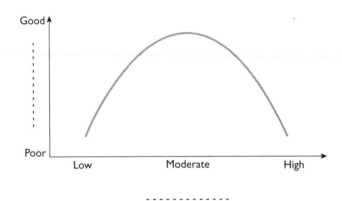

(d) **Describe and evaluate two psychological techniques for improving performance in sport. In evaluating, include at least one comparison point.** (12 marks)

✏ **(a)** This question is asking about participation but could have been about performance. Watch for those two terms to see which one a question is about. This question is unusual, as there is no clear 'injunction' word like 'outline' or 'describe'. It asks how personality traits might explain sporting participation. This is not quite the same as asking you to describe the personality theory, as the answer needs also to show how the personality might affect participation. For example, it is thought that different sports 'attract' different personalities.

(b) This is a fairly standard format for an exam question and is likely to involve 2 marks for the strength and 2 for the weakness. Give both in enough detail to make them clear and then add some elaboration in each case for the additional mark.

(c) The inverted U is usually shown as a diagram and this question is asking you to label two variables. The lines indicate where the answer should be written. There is only 1 mark because once you have added one term, the other must go in the other space.

(d) This is an essay question, so refer to the comments on question 3(a) in Section 3 of Health Psychology (p. 75) for more information about how to answer an essay question and how an essay answer is marked. The marking uses levels so you do not have to give a certain number of points — it is the quality of your answer that gets credit as well as the quantity. The question needs an equal focus on describing and evaluating each of the two techniques, so allow about three or four marking points for each part. Make sure there is one point where the two techniques are compared.

■ ■ ■

Answers

(a) Eysenck suggested that there are two main dimensions with regard to personality — the introversion/extroversion dimension and the neurotic/stable dimension. Studies tend to show that extroverts seek exercise behaviour more than introverts, ✓ supposedly because they have a strong nervous system and their ARAS damps it down and so it is their natural tendency to seek stimulation. ✓ So for sports that need a lot of exercise, you would expect to find more extroverts, and for sports that need precision rather than exercise (such as shooting), you might find more introverts. ✓ Studies support these ideas. Neuroticism seems to mean less likelihood of doing exercise, so there should be more stable personalities undertaking sport that requires a lot of exercise. ✓

📝 There are four marking points here — the point is credited (such as that extroverts seek exercise more) and then the elaboration is credited as well. This is one way to increase marks — by adding depth rather than breadth. Breadth in this question would involve giving a lot of effects, while depth involves giving fewer effects and elaborating more.

(b) One strength of the achievement motivation theory is that it links well to the idea of socialisation as a factor in sporting performance and participation because both theories use the idea of positive reinforcement. ✓ Achievement motivation theory suggests that fear of failure is a factor, and fear of failure is likely to be higher if someone is not rewarded for some sporting behaviour, so they lack confidence in that area. Positive reinforcement should mean lower fear of failure, which means higher achievement motivation. Socialisation as a theory suggests that people do again what they are rewarded for by parents and others in society, so the two theories reinforce one another, which is a strength. ✓

A weakness of achievement motivation theory is that self-report data is often gathered as evidence, using questionnaires and attitude scales. Such data are often unreliable, as attitude can depend on mood and this can vary over different days and times. ✓ It might be useful to get some other data, for example, from others who know the individual, to try to validate the data, or perhaps repeat the study at a different time or day to find test–retest reliability. ✓

✍ Both the strength and the weakness get the 2 marks, though the strength is explained in perhaps more detail than is needed. It is, however, not an easy strength to explain and it is better to give too much detail than to lose the second mark by not making the point clearly enough.

(c)

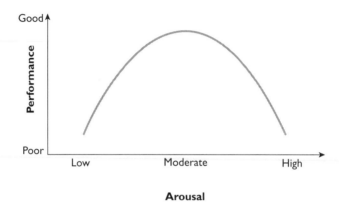

Arousal

✍ Both terms are in the correct spaces so 1 mark is given. If only one term was correct there would be 0 marks, as there would be if both terms were incorrect or there was a blank space.

(d) One way to improve performance is using imagery and there are five ways to use imagery. Visualising is one type of imagery, but there are others that are also useful, such as acting out (kinaesthetic) and auditory (e.g. hearing the crowd). The five ways to use imagery include cognitive specific imagery which is about learning a skill, cognitive general imagery which is about learning a strategy, learning self-confidence (motivational), learning to control anxiety (also motivational) and learning to focus on goals. The idea is to imagine a scenario and to step into it to practise it, so you have already experienced it when it happens. The aim is to imagine succeeding and this helps you to succeed, for example in achieving a certain goal or mastering a certain skill (e.g. achieving a really good score in archery). Visualising a tennis shot before you play it can be useful.

Another way to improve performance is to set goals, which help to focus on what is to be achieved and how to achieve it. There are three main principles with regard to goal-setting. Setting difficult goals is more successful with regard to higher performance than setting goals that are too easy and so do not motivate someone to repeat the performance. Another principle is that specific goals lead to higher performance, presumably because they are easier to focus on than general goals and there can be a step-by-step road to success. The third principle is about feedback. Feedback is very important so that the individual knows what they have achieved, how effective their achievement has been, and possibly how to improve. One similarity between using goal-setting and using imagery is that for goal-setting, the individual would have to imagine the goal they want to achieve in order to plan the steps to achieve it, and they would tend to use more than one of the five functions of imagery, including cognitive specific (specific plans of how to achieve) and motivational (imagining success to see how to reach it).

This answer is very good regarding description of two techniques for improving performance, and there is one comparison point as asked. However, there is no other evaluation, so this answer would be in the middle band and achieve around 7 of the 12 marks. The level of the description is high and terms are used appropriately (though the names of the five functions are not all known), but without evaluation around half of the essay is missing. This shows the need to focus on the whole question. Evaluation points that could be added include:

- Mellalieu et al. (2006) showed the success of goal-setting in rugby when participants who set specific measurable goals succeeded in improving their performance.
- Although much of the research has been laboratory-based so the findings tend to lack validity, Mellalieu et al. (2006) was a field study carried out with rugby players who applied goal-setting in real matches.
- Feltz and Landers (1983) found that mental practice improved performance more than no practice but not as much as physical practice, so using imagery has some success but is not the only answer to improving performance.
- There is criticism of methods used to study imagery, as the skills studied tend to be novice skills (learning the sport can be the easiest to measure) and so there might not be validity in applying the findings to more practised sportspeople.

Studies in detail

From Cottrell et al. (1968), Koivula (1995), Craft et al. (2003) and Boyd and Munroe (2003), choose two studies and compare their research methodology. (6 marks)

📝 You will have studied at least two of the studies listed in the question, including the compulsory study Boyd and Munroe (2003), so focus on the two you know best. Think of their main research methodology and then, using the two studies, contrast the methods, or point out areas where they are the same. You could give some general points as well, such as saying that both used ethical methods, and explaining how. If the two methods are the same in general, there are probably ways in which they are different in practice, so you can focus on those.

■ ■ ■

Answer

Boyd and Munroe (2003) used questionnaires and so did Koivula (1995) in her study of gender and sport — in fact, both used two questionnaires and both wanted to see how the answers in the two questionnaires compared with one another in some way. ✓ Boyd and Munroe (2003) gave one questionnaire to track and field athletes and the other to climbers to compare their use of imagery. Koivula (1995) used the BSRI to get participants to rate themselves with regard to masculinity or femininity, and then gave the same participants another questionnaire to find out about how they rated the appropriateness of different sports with regard to gender. (✓ — elaboration)

Boyd and Munroe (2003) used an independent groups design (track and field athletes versus climbers) and Koivula (1995) used a repeated measures design (the same participants, to correlate view of sport with regard to gender and view of themselves with regard to gender). (✓✓ — double tick, as a lot of detail in this point)

All the questionnaires used a 7-point Likert scale in the answers so the question-naires were all self-rating ones and all used the same idea for the number of points in the ratings. ✓ Both used a standardised questionnaire, at least for one of the ones they used. Boyd and Munroe used the standardised SIQ (sport imagery ques-tionnaire) and Koivula used the BSRI (Bem sex role inventory). ✓ This meant that the questionnaire had been tested for reliability, which helped the reliability of their findings. For the second questionnaire, both had written up their own or at least had amended a standardised one. ✓ Boyd and Munroe simply adapted the SIQ to be very similar for the climbers, but Koivula drew up a questionnaire to ask about lists of sports and whether they were 'more masculine than feminine' and so on, so Koivula's second questionnaire was more different from Boyd and Munroe's. Boyd and Munroe were trying to keep their survey the same between their two indepen-dent groups, whereas Koivula had two different questionnaires to give to the same group of people. ✓

There are a lot of marking points here and some thorough comparison points. This answer clearly earns full marks. It is important to know a lot of detail about what are called in the course 'studies in detail' so that you can answer questions like this one. It is a hard question, carrying a lot of marks. Such questions are not likely to appear in every paper, but they are possible, so be ready for them.

10

Evidence in practice: key issue and practical

The following questions concern the practical you carried out when studying sport psychology. You will have carried out either a content analysis focusing on a key issue or a summary analysis of two sources focusing on a topic covered within the application. Answer the following questions with that analysis or summary in mind.

(a) How did you choose the topic for your summary analysis of two sources or for your content analysis? (2 marks)

(b) Outline what you did when carrying out your analysis or summary. (3 marks)

(c) Explain one problem you found with your practical and how you addressed the problem (or how you could have addressed the problem). (3 marks)

   (a) This question asks you to explain your focus in your practical and why you chose that focus. Answer specifically (do not just say that you chose it because it was your key issue). The marking is done using levels, not point by point. Questions on practicals are generally marked using levels because it is hard to predict what candidates will write about — the marking is more about quality than quantity or getting the 'right answer'.

   (b) For this question give some elements of the procedure, which can include how you did the content analysis or how you chose the articles and summarised them. Answers to questions about the practical use levels marking, not point-by-point marking, so there are no ticks in the answer below. Answers are marked for quality as well as quantity.

   (c) For this question, if there was a problem and you addressed it, give that as the answer. However, if you cannot think of a problem you addressed, give a problem with the practical that you can now think of and then discuss how you could have addressed it.

■ ■ ■

Answers

(a) I carried out a content analysis that looked at my key issue and I chose my key issue from a list for the course. I studied Koivula (1995), who looked at gender and sport, so my key issue was gender and sport. Also, I am male and enjoy reading sport pages of newspapers, so I had already noticed that much of the coverage looks at male sport, and I wanted to carry out a study to look at this more formally.

   This is a thorough answer well worth the 2 marks. There are a few reasons given. They include the sensible reason that the key issue was from a list for the course, but give more than this — that choice of topic had to be picked from a list, so say why. It is useful to have chosen something interesting as the key issue so that you can explain why it interested you (and also in order to study something that interests you).

(b) For my content analysis I bought a newspaper that had a lot of sport at the back — I chose *The Independent*. Then, using two coloured highlighter pens, I highlighted any reference to male sportspeople in one colour and any reference to female sportspeople in the other colour, so that I had a visual pattern. Then I needed to count instances, so I counted the number of highlighted parts. However, I realised that a name was repeated a lot so I chose instead to measure the column inches for the areas that were highlighted (the whole article, not just the name) and counted the inches for the 'male' highlighting compared with the 'female' highlighting. I then had a list of numbers to total for male coverage and a list of numbers for female coverage, and I added up the numbers to get a score for each. It was clear even visually, however, that there was very little 'female' coverage at all compared with 'male' coverage, so it was not hard to analyse the data.

> 🖉 There is enough here for the 3 marks as the answer is detailed and clear. There is a logical progression through the answer, which shows the reader clearly understood what was carried out.

(c) Answer one
I needed to count instances of male and female sportspeople mentioned in the paper so I highlighted each in a different colour and counted the number of highlighted parts. However, I realised that a name was repeated a lot so I chose instead to measure the column inches for the areas that were highlighted (the whole article not just the name) and counted the inches for the 'male' highlighted articles compared with the 'female' highlighted articles. I could have counted the name more than once as this still represented male sport coverage, but I preferred to count column inches, as otherwise the study would have been more about how often a name was mentioned than how much coverage there was of male and female sport.

> 🖉 This answer is probably enough for the 3 marks as the problem is explained, the way it was addressed is explained and the reason why it was a problem is clear.

Answer two
I only used one newspaper on one day, so it is hard to generalise from my finding that there was a lot more coverage of male sportspeople (and, therefore, male sport) than of female sport. It could be that some male sportspeople were 'in the news' for some reason rather than that they were in the paper because it was male not female sport. Perhaps, for example, athletics or swimming would have given more equal numbers of males and females, whereas the time of year I chose featured football and rugby more. I should have repeated the study on different days using the same newspaper or using different newspapers as well and at different times of year. Also I could have repeated the study using a different medium such as television to see if there was more 'male' coverage. This would improve the reliability and generalisability of the results.

This is a thorough answer that looks more at an overall problem with the study rather than a specific one with the procedure. This answer is different but just as useful as the other answer, and would also get full marks.